DATE DUE

DEC 07 '94			
APR 26 '95			
APR 2 9 1999			
OCT 1 2 2000			
NOV 2 2 2010			

HIGHSMITH   # 45220

D1403143

Suicide in Later Life

Suicide in Later Life

Recognizing the Warning Signs

Nancy J. Osgood

LEXINGTON BOOKS
An Imprint of Macmillan, Inc.
NEW YORK

Maxwell Macmillan Canada
TORONTO

Maxwell Macmillan International
NEW YORK · OXFORD · SINGAPORE · SYDNEY

Tennessee Tech Library
Cookeville, TN

Library of Congress Cataloging-in-Publication Data
Osgood, Nancy J.
    Suicide in later life: recognizing the warning signs/ Nancy J.
Osgood.
        p. cm.
    Includes bibliographical references and index.
    ISBN 0-669-21214-8
    1. Aged—United States—Suicidal behavior. 2. Suicide—United
States—Prevention. I. Title.
HV6545.2.0845 1992
362.2′8′0846—dc20   92-13865
                                                            CIP

Copyright © 1992 by Lexington Books
An Imprint of Macmillan, Inc.

All rights reserved. No part of this book may be reproduced
or transmitted in any form or by any means, electronic or
mechanical, including photocopying, recording, or by any
information storage and retrieval system, without permission
in writing from the Publisher.

Lexington Books
An Imprint of Macmillan, Inc.
866 Third Avenue, New York, N.Y. 10022

Maxwell Macmillan Canada, Inc.
1200 Eglinton Avenue East
Suite 200
Don Mills, Ontario M3C 3N1

Macmillan, Inc. is part of the Maxwell Communication
Group of Companies.

Printed in the United States of America

printing number

1   2   3   4   5   6   7   8   9   10

The author and the publisher gratefully acknowledge permission to reprint excerpts from the following sources:

Simone de Beauvoir, *The Coming of Age*. New York: G. P. Putnam's Sons, 1972.

Daniel Callahan, *Setting Limits*. New York: Simon and Schuster, 1987.

The Complete Poems of Emily Dickinson, edited by Thomas H. Johnson. Boston: Little, Brown and Company, 1924.

Viktor Frankl, *Man's Search for Meaning*. Boston: Beacon Press, 1959.

The Poetry of Robert Frost, edited by Edward Connery Lathem. Copyright 1969 by Holt, Rinehart and Winston. Acknowledgment is made to Henry Holt and Company, Inc., New York, N.Y. 10011.

The Satires of Juvenal, edited by R. Humphries. Bloomington: Indiana University Press, 1958.

McLeish, J. A. B. *The Ulyssean Adult: Creativity in the Middle and Later Years*. New York: McGraw-Hill, 1976. Acknowledgment is made to McGraw-Hill Book Co., New York, N.Y. 10020.

M. Miller, *Suicide after Sixty: The Final Alternative*. Copyright 1979 by Springer Publishing Company, Inc., New York, N.Y. 10012. Used by permission.

R. Müller, *Most of All, They Taught Me Happiness*. New York: Doubleday, 1978. Quoted with permission.

Florida P. Scott-Maxwell. *The Measure of My Days*. New York: Knopf, 1968.

Bernie S. Siegel, *Love, Medicine, and Miracles*. Copyright 1986 by Bernie S. Siegel, S. Korman, and A. Schiff, Trustees of the Bernard S. Siegel, M. D. Children's Trust. Reprinted by permission of HarperCollins Publishers.

William Styron, *Darkness Visible: A Memoir of Madness*. New York: Random House, 1990.

Dylan Thomas, *Poems of Dylan Thomas*. Copyright 1952 by Dylan Thomas. Reprinted by permission of New Directions Publishing Corporation.

Dylan Thomas, *The Poems*. London: Dent. Reprinted by permission.

The Poetic and Dramatic Works of Alfred Lord Tennyson. Copyright 1898 by Houghton Mifflin Company.

Acknowledgment is made of permission to reproduce the following cartoons:

"*These pills should help your amnesia.*" Copyright 1983; reprinted courtesy of Bunny Hoest and *Parade Magazine*.

"*Bridge out.*" Copyright Bruce Cochran and *Playboy Magazine*.

"*Grandma, do wrinkles hurt?*" Reprinted by permission of Jerry Marcus.

The data for age group 65 and older in Figure 1–1, Figure 1–2, and Table 1–1 are derived from the Appendix in N. J. Osgood and J. McIntosh, *Suicide and the Elderly: An Annotated Bibliography and Review* (Westport, Conn.: Greenwood Press, 1986). The data for recent years were calculated by Dr. John McIntosh from National Center for Health Statistics data.

Lovingly dedicated to my father,
Jack Luttrell

Contents

Figures and Tables

FIGURES

TABLES

Preface

Growing old in our youth-oriented society is often a tragedy. Many old people are poor or can barely make ends meet, living on meager pensions or social security. Some live in substandard housing, isolated and alone. Some are ill. Many never receive visits from children or grandchildren, who have moved away and are busy with their own lives. Rejected and abandoned by a society that sees them as ugly and disgusting, nonproductive and useless, an economic burden to younger members, many elders in America prefer death to old age.

Compared to other age groups, those age 65 and older have the highest rate of suicide in the United States. Elders have a suicide rate that is more than 50 percent higher than the suicide rate for the general population. For many, the golden years are tarnished.

The idyllic picture of later life as a quiet, peaceful time when we are free to relax and enjoy ourselves, spend time with family and friends, and travel and engage in interesting hobbies and activities is not the reality for everyone. There is a dark side far removed from that glossy golf course view of aging. Sickness, loneliness, isolation, depression, and despair are too often companions in later life. Hopes and dreams of a well-deserved life of luxury, to be enjoyed with spouse and friends, are often shattered when a husband or wife dies or when serious illness strikes. Loss of important roles in the work and family spheres and in the community can create a void. Suddenly everything meaningful and worthwhile is gone, and the older individual is left alone to restructure his or her world and find new sources of meaning.

Old people in the United States face prejudice and negative stereotypes every day. Myths abound about old people and old age. We think of old people as cranky and grumpy, sexless and senile. We associate aging with decline, disease, decrepitude, and death. Some other cultures honor and respect elders for their knowledge and wisdom; elders in the United States are often ignored or treated disrespectfully. American society does not provide a wide array of valuable roles and positions for older people. Instead, they become just another throwaway in our throwaway culture.

A growing segment of America's aging population is lonely, isolated, and despairing, and some elders are choosing suicide as the solution to later life's problems. Even rich and famous elders who live glamorous lives and seem to "have it all" are committing suicide. Perhaps the best example is Ernest Hemingway. He was one of America's most famous writers, had a loving and devoted wife, and had fame and fortune, but at age 62 Hemingway took a gun and blew his brains out. Neither money nor modern medicine could save him.

This book portrays realistically the problem of later-life suicide. I rely on published suicide statistics to outline the dimensions of the problem and to highlight past and future trends, and I provide case studies to dramatize the plight of the vulnerable elderly and to show how suicidal elders feel.

In *Suicide in Later Life* I offer a discussion of the major causes of later-life suicide by drawing on my personal and professional research and experience, professional literature, and case illustrations from a variety of sources. I am looking for ways to prevent suicide among the elderly. How do we as a nation change our attitudes and alter our behavior toward elders to reduce their risk of suicide? I offer my own and others' solutions in this book, presenting ideal as well as more realisitc possibilities.

Health care rationing, cost containment, euthanasia, assisted suicide, and the right to die are hot topics of debate among ethicists and philosophers, medical professionals, legal professionals, and policymakers throughout government. At the highest levels of government there is talk of rationing health care on the basis of age, denying older individuals the most expensive life-sustaining medical technologies. In medical and religious circles there is growing acceptance of the idea of the right to die, especially for the old. As economic resources become scarcer, we have witnessed a growing climate of opinion that views the old as an economic burden on the rest of society and increasingly accepts suicide among older people. Are we on the verge of a new era in which we are willing to sacrifice the lives of some of our "less productive" members for the so-called good of the rest of society? These and other ethical issues are examined in *Suicide in Later Life*.

One of my primary intentions in writing this book is to provoke thought about attitudes and beliefs about aging and old people and to examine societal attitudes and public policy toward the elderly. We all will be old some day. Cultural attitudes and societal policies now in place will help to shape future attitudes and policies. What kind of society do we want to live in—and die in—when we are old?

1

The Tragedy of Suicide
in Later Life

In describing the situation facing many older people at the end of life, Simone de Beauvoir (1972) wrote:

> Above all, even if the old person is struck by no particular misfortune, he has usually either lost his reasons for living or he has discovered their absence. When the world alters or displays itself in such a way that remaining in it becomes unbearable a young man can hope for change; an old man cannot. All that is left for him is to wish for death. (p. 26).

Suicidal elders live in all different types of settings and come from all walks of life. Some are nobodies; others are famous. Some live transient lives as skid row derelicts; others live in mansions in Beverly Hills and West Palm Beach. Some live in their own homes with their spouses; others live alone with no daily contact with friends or relatives or in nursing homes or adult homes. Many live lives of quiet desperation—isolated, lonely, depressed, abandoned, and rejected. Many are physically ill and in pain. All of those who commit suicide have decided that life is not worth living. The following cases dramatically portray the tragedy of suicide in later life.

Ernest Hemingway: Even the Famous Kill Themselves

On July 2, 1961, at the age of 62, Ernest Hemingway fatally shot himself at home where he lived with his wife, Mary. He had just been released from the Mayo Clinic, where he had been treated with electroconvulsive therapy for severe depression, delusions, and obsessions.

Hemingway was reared in the Midwest by a critical and domineering mother who required absolute obedience from her son. His father, a weak, ineffectual man, also was dominated by Hemingway's mother. Hemingway, rejecting his parents, left home as a teenager to serve as a soldier and was seriously wounded fighting in Fossalta, Italy. His father, a physician, committed suicide when Hemingway was 29. When Hemingway came to claim his inheritance, his mother told him that if he ever disobeyed her, he would regret it all of his life, just as his father had.

Hemingway probably suffered throughout his adult life from the ill effects of being reared in such an unhealthy family atmosphere. He had difficulty maintaining close, intimate relationships and was known for his public humiliation and rejection of close friends who at some point failed to meet his expectations. He had difficulty establishing sound marriages; he married four times and was unfaithful to all of his wives. He sought out independent, successful career women for partners, some of whom were older than he, which might suggest a basic dependence on women and an injured sense of personal competence. Women provided Hemingway's inspiration and his audience. Two recurrent themes in Hemingway's works are homosexuality and venereal disease—both related to the male's fear and rejection of women. Hemingway was a heavy drinker throughout his adult life.

Hemingway strove to cultivate an image of himself as the super-competent "macho man." He boxed, hunted big game, fished, and fought in the bull ring. He was fondly known to friends and fans as "Papa" Hemingway. His closest friends described him as shy and sensitive.

Hemingway had a brilliant literary career, writing such well-known novels as *The Old Man and the Sea,* for which he won a Pulitzer Prize in 1954; *Across the River and into the Trees; Death in the Afternoon; For Whom the Bell Tolls; Green Hills of Africa;* and *To Have and Have Not.* He was close friends with famous writers, artists, movie stars, and matadors. He traveled extensively, spending considerable time in Key West, Havana, New York City, Paris, and finally Ketchum, Idaho.

Hemingway experienced emotional turmoil, serious accidents,

and frequent illness as an adult. In 1951, Hemingway experienced the death of his first grandson, his mother, an ex-wife, his housemaid (who committed suicide), his best friend, and his publisher. In his later years, Hemingway's physical abilities and literary talents began to fail. In 1954 he was in two plane crashes in Africa and sustained a ruptured kidney, internal injuries, a concussion, double vision, and a badly burned left hand, the last an especially serious blow, since he was left-handed. After the crashes, he was in physical pain and began drinking even more than in the past. He became concerned about weight gain, high cholesterol, and elevated blood pressure. He suffered from a skin condition that caused his skin to flake off. And Hemingway became increasingly nervous and irritable during the last years of his life. He developed an obsession with women's hair as he began to lose his own hair.

Shortly after the plane crashes, the news media pressured Hemingway, asking for interviews, taking photographs, and writing stories about him—interruptions that made it difficult for him to write. His publishers were after him to produce another prize-winning novel, although he was already committed to writing several magazine pieces. The stress aggravated his physical problems and contributed to his heavy drinking. His years of heavy drinking may have contributed to his inability to produce good-quality written work.

As his health worsened, his physician advised him to maintain a strict diet, not to drink, and to give up sexual intercourse—admonitions that were devastating to a man who had always been vigorous and in complete control of his life. In response, Hemingway withdrew, eating more meals alone in his room, refusing to travel or engage in activities that had always provided great pleasure. He kept drinking, he argued more with his wife, and he was often depressed.

By 1951, when he was 52 years old, Hemingway began to lose through death many people who were important to him. He also knew he could not keep returning to his beloved Cuba, where anti-American sentiment was growing stronger. He was involved in numerous legal battles related to his publications and to movies based on his works.

Hemingway's eyesight began to fail from keratitis sicca, a dry eye syndrome affecting the cornea. Doctors told him if medication did not control the disease, he would go blind. Writing became more difficult. He began to lose confidence in his ability to do good work and to complete the manuscripts he had committed to finish. His writing also was attacked by critics, a blow for a man to whom writing was his life. He suffered more from depression and delusions and had hallucinations. He believed he was going to be financially ruined and had delusions that his wife was stealing his money. He developed a persecution complex and thought that his friends, his wife, and physician, and even complete strangers were "out to get him." He imagined he was being followed and spied on by federal agents. In the late 1950s he attempted suicide using one of his guns; the attempt failed.

After being treated with electroconvulsive therapy at the Mayo Clinic in Rochester, Minnesota, Hemingway returned home. At age 62, before he shot himself fatally, he confided to his good friend A. E. Hotchner (1966) that "man is not made for defeat. He can be destroyed but not defeated." Apparently Hemingway chose self-destruction to avoid physical and literary defeat.

Bruno Bettelheim: Suicide Happens in Institutions Too

On March 13, 1990, at the age of 86, Bruno Bettelheim, a world-famous psychologist, committed suicide by placing a plastic bag over his head. He lived in a Maryland nursing home.

Bruno Bettelheim was born in Vienna in 1903 of Jewish parents. By the time he was 14, he had read Freud's works on psychoanalysis and later pursued a career in psychology specializing in child autism. He wrote extensively on child psychology. His best-known works are *The Uses of Enchantment* and *On Learning to Read*.

In 1938 Bettelheim was incarcerated in concentration camps, first Buchenwald and then Dachau. Eleanor Roosevelt was instrumental in gaining his release. After his release from the camps, Bettelheim immigrated to the United States, where he married a social worker and pursued a long and productive life as a scholar at the University of Chicago. He spent his life working with, researching, and writing about autistic children and disturbed youth. Students of Bettelheim describe him as a tough teacher, strongly opinionated, and fiercely defensive of his own ideas and positions.

As he aged, Bettelheim confronted many losses. When his wife died after forty-three years of marriage, he was devastated. A brief live-in arrangement with a son ended when difficulties arose between them, and Bettelheim moved into a condominium, where he lived alone. Three years after his wife died, Bettelheim had a stroke that left him unable to think and process information as he had earlier. As he began to lose his mental abilities, Bettelheim's depression deepened.

Still in control of his own life, Bettelheim decided to enter a retirement home where he could have help meeting his physical needs. Shortly after the move, he realized he had made a mistake. Institutionalization represented a major loss of independence to a man who had been independent throughout his adult life. Bettelheim feared even further loss of health and independence. Afraid and lonely, he ended his life. His friends see his final act not as a surrender but as an act of mastery over his life.

Paul and Lois Martin: Some Marriages Have Deadly Love Pacts

On June 1, 1983, Lois Martin, 71, and her husband, Paul, 79, were discovered by their daughter in their condominium in a retirement community in southern California. Both were dead. A half-empty bottle of whiskey and an empty bottle of tranquilizers near the couple were evidence that the Martins had committed suicide together. Mrs. Martin was a retired psychologist and public school counselor; her husband had been a college president.

The Martins, who met as professor and student in college, had been married for nearly fifty years. They had two grown children: a daughter who was a professor and a son who was a dentist. They had regular contact with their grandchildren.

Lois and Paul had been busy professionals. Paul Martin briefly served as an officer in the U.S. Marine Corps. Lois was the socialite of the couple, while her husband was a reserved scholar who preferred quiet time and privacy.

A lover of the outdoors, Paul Martin spent most of his days landscaping and gardening after he retired at age 65. His wife retired five years later when she turned 62. In poor health for several years, she had difficulty breathing and tired easily. A year after she retired, Lois Martin was diagnosed as having emphysema.

During the last decade of their lives, the Martins went downhill physically. As her emphysema worsened, every breath was an effort.

She was on oxygen around the clock. Cooking a simple meal or sweeping the floor became too much for her, a loss for a woman who had been a gourmet cook and a meticulous housekeeper. Her socializing days were gone, and she became isolated. During her last year, Lois was unable to walk or talk without severe breathing difficulty.

Paul too suffered serious physical losses during his final years. He had to give up driving and gardening because he suffered from dizzy spells. His heart enlarged, and his arteries hardened. He had a minor stroke and was hospitalized briefly. He lost his vision and his hearing. The heart medications he took had numerous side effects, including drowsiness, nausea, and severe muscle cramps that greatly reduced his capacity to work and play. During the last two years of life, Paul Martin never dressed or went out of his apartment except to see doctors.

The Martins became invalids, confined to a tiny apartment to live out a life of pain and misery. Confronted with what they viewed as a hopeless situation, Lois attempted suicide by slashing her wrists; the attempt failed.

When Paul learned of his wife's attempted suicide, he expressed his wish to die with her. The couple began actively seeking information on how to complete a suicide. They contacted Derek Humphry at the Hemlock Society, an organization that promotes suicide, especially in cases of terminal illness, read books on suicide, sought advice from physicians, and elicited help from their children.

The Martins carefully planned their double suicide. They paid their bills, put their business and legal affairs in order, and said goodbye to their children and grandchildren. The nurse who provided around-the-clock care was given her birthday night off and assured that someone else would be coming in for the evening. Alone, Paul and Lois prepared for their deaths. Around midnight, after eating a meal together and talking for hours, Lois crushed the tranquilizers and mixed them in whiskey. They drank the mixture and died.

James Tiptree, Jr.: First Murder, Then Suicide

On May 5, 1987, in McLean, Virginia, nationally known science fiction writer Alice Sheldon, who wrote under the pseudonym James Tiptree, Jr., shot her husband in the head. Then she put the gun in her mouth and pulled the trigger. Alice Sheldon was 71. Her husband, Huntington, was 84. The murder-suicide shocked the literary community.

Alice Sheldon, born in Chicago in 1915, grew up in Africa and India. She earned a Ph.D. in experimental psychology and spent much of her adult life conducting experimental research in psychology and working for the U.S. government. She met her husband while employed with the Central Intelligence Agency, where Huntington was an analyst. For most of their married life, they lived in a large, secluded wooded lot across from the CIA headquarters in northern Virginia. The couple were described by friends as avid nature lovers.

Alice Sheldon took up writing in her 50s and wrote science fiction books and short stories; her first story was published in 1968. She used a pseudonym to conceal her identity, but when her mother, Mary Hastings Bradley, a well-known geographer and travel author, died, Alice Sheldon's identity was disclosed. This unwanted revelation in addition to the death of her mother plunged her into a deep depression.

Alice Sheldon wrote many well-known books and award-winning stories, including "Birth of a Salesman," "Warm Worlds and Otherwise," "How to Have an Absolutely Hilarious Heart Attack," "Tales of the Quintana Roo," and *Brightness Falls from the Air*. One book written late in her career is entitled *Love Is the Plan, the Plan Is Death*. She was described as one of the finest science fiction writers of the 1970s. One critic referred to her as "brilliant, powerful, unique."

In their later years, both Sheldons suffered from serious physical health problems. He had severe heart disease, emphysema, and pneumonia and had been blind for many years. She had chronic lung disease and had had heart surgery, including coronary artery bypass and a mitral valve replacement. The mail carrier who saw the couple every day described their lives as filled with illness and pain. As they became sicker and frailer, he said, they became withdrawn and reclusive.

According to the authorities who investigated the deaths, the couple apparently had a suicide pact, agreeing to die if living became too difficult for one or both of them. Alice Sheldon had threatened suicide for the final twenty years of her life. As quoted from the records of the medical examiner, Alice Sheldon wrote to a friend in 1976, "I had always meant to take myself off the scene gracefully about now while I am still me. And now I find I can't, because to do it would mean leaving him alone, and I can't bring myself to put a bullet through that sleeping head—to take him, too, when he doesn't want to go." On the day of the murder-suicide in 1987, she telephoned her lawyer to advise him she had shot her husband and was going to shoot herself. When police arrived, they found husband and wife lying in bed. He was covered with a comforter; his head rested on a blood-soaked pillow. His wife, who was on top of the cover with a towel wrapped around her face, had one small line of blood trickling down her face. She held his hand with her right hand. In her left, which lay on her chest, was a revolver. After their deaths, one friend told a news reporter, "They lived a beautiful life, very loving." Another described them as "very vital, intelligent people. They were finding life very fragile right now."

Emily and Roswell Gilbert: A Life Sentence for Mercy Killing

On March 4, 1985, in their tenth-story condominium in Fort Lauderdale, Florida, a retired engineer named Roswell Gilbert, 76, loaded a pistol and shot two bullets into the brain of his ailing 73-year-old wife, Emily. The couple had been married more than fifty years. On May 9, 1985, after a jury of twelve deliberated for just over four hours, Gilbert was convicted of first-degree murder. Broward County circuit court judge Thomas Coker, Jr., in what is probably the most publicized case of mercy killing in history, sentenced Gilbert to twenty-five years in prison with no chance of parole. But on August 2, 1990, the governor of Florida granted Gilbert clemency, and at age 81, Gilbert, suffering from heart and lung disease, was released from prison in Lake Butler, Florida. A crowd of onlookers watched him walk out of the prison with his daughter holding his hand.

Roswell and Emily Gilbert, who were married in 1936, retired to Spain. After living there only a few years, Roswell noticed that Emily was having memory lapses and was sometimes confused, and she began complaining of pain in her back.

The couple returned to the United States in 1978, purchasing the condominium just north of Fort Lauderdale, because Roswell thought his wife would receive better medical care in the United States. Emily was diagnosed with osteoporosis and Alzheimer's disease.

Between 1978 and 1985, Emily's conditioned worsened. The back pain grew progressively worse; her spine shortened by more than two inches due to bone fractures. Painkillers prescribed by her doctor did not relieve her severe physical pain. The Alzheimer's disease also progressed. As her mind faded, she became totally dependent on Roswell, who bathed and dressed her, brushed her hair, flossed her teeth, and cooked for her.

As Emily became progressively more mentally and physically debilitated, friends came by less often to visit. Social isolation and the burden of constantly caring for his wife took their toll on Gilbert. Frustrated, drained, and hopeless, Gilbert sought custodial care for his ailing wife. He was unsuccessful, and the total burden of her care fell back on him. Exhausted from lack of sleep and physical and emotional strain, Gilbert decided to end Emily's suffering—and his own.

After he shot his wife, Gilbert claimed he committed the act out of mercy to end his wife's pain and misery. After he heard the verdict of the jury and the sentence, Gilbert said, "Justice is on my side, but the law is on somebody else's side." Gilbert claimed he acted out of love and had done nothing wrong. When he left the Florida prison five years later, Gilbert said publicly for the first time that he was wrong to have killed his wife.

Although these cases represent tragic deaths of well-known individuals and couples, the majority of suicides, double suicides, murder-suicides, and assisted suicides of older adults go unnoticed. Reported or ignored, such deaths attest that "for many older Americans old age is a tragedy, a period of quiet despair, deprivation, desolation, and muted rage" (Butler, 1975, p. 2).

The Problem of Suicide in Later Life

In 1988, 6,363 individuals aged 65 and older were recorded as having committed suicide. Every day 17 older adults—or 1 every 93 minutes—choose to die. Clearly death by suicide in the elderly represents a major public health problem. Suicide is the thirteenth leading cause of death amongst the elderly, a group for whom deaths from nearly all causes are the highest, and the first and leading cause of unnecessary death. Deaths by suicide, however, potentially are the most preventable type of death.

A major misconception is that suicide is primarily a phenomenon of adolescence. Until recently most research and media attention in the United States has focused on the problem of suicide among teenagers. The reality is that suicide is primarily a problem of later life, and the elderly are the group most at risk. In fact, the suicide rate for the elderly is 50 percent higher than that of the young or the nation as a whole. We live in a youth-oriented society where the social problem of elderly suicide has been virtually ignored.

Many teenagers attempt suicide as a gesture to get attention from or to manipulate others; they are crying for help. Older adults, on the other hand, are deadly serious about killing themselves; they are suicide completers. It is estimated that there are 10 to 20 suicidal attempts for every suicide completion for the population as a whole. Ratios for the young are as high as 200 to 1; for the elderly, the ratio is 4 to 1 (McIntosh, 1985).

Older adults are more likely than teenagers to die by their own hand for a variety of reasons. First, older adults often use guns, the most lethal method of suicide; teenagers choose less violent methods, such as wrist slashing and drug overdoses. Additionally, compared to teenagers, older people have more medical problems and are more vulnerable physically; they are more likely to die from engaging in a suicidal act. Finally, older adults, unlike teenagers, take measures to ensure that their suicide will not be discovered and interrupted.

Changing Rates of Suicide

Data from the National Center for Health Statistics reveal interesting changes in suicide rates by age group over time. The rate of suicide among individuals aged 65 and older has been steadily increasing since 1980. That increase comes after a half-century of decline in the rate of suicide for that age group. The rate of suicide for those aged 65 and over steadily declined from 45.3 per 100,000 in 1933 to 17.65 per 100,000 in 1980, a 61 percent decline. During the 1980s there was a reversal of that trend; the rate of elderly suicide steadily climbed every year, except one, from 17.65 per 100,000 in 1980 to 20.9 per 100,000 in 1988. (In 1989 it decreased slightly.) The rate of suicide among the elderly increased 25 percent between 1981 and

1988, and the total number of suicides for older people rose 40 percent during that time. In contrast to the steady increase in the rate of elderly suicide, there has been no increase or a very slight one in the suicide rate for teenagers and other age groups and for the nation as a whole. The national suicide rate for all ages in 1989 was 12.2 per 100,000. The suicide rate for teenagers peaked in 1977 and has declined since then, to 13.3 per 100,000 in 1989. Today elderly males have a suicide rate four times the national average. (For a comparison of suicide rates for older adults, teenagers, and the U.S. population, see figures 1–1 and 1–2 and table 1–1). The statistics give rise to two questions: why did the rate of suicide for the elderly decrease for fifty years, and why is the rate now steadily increasing?

Why the Increase?

Several researchers interested in the phenomenon of suicide in later life have speculated about why the rate of suicide among those age 65 and over decreased between 1933 and 1980. Although the rise in

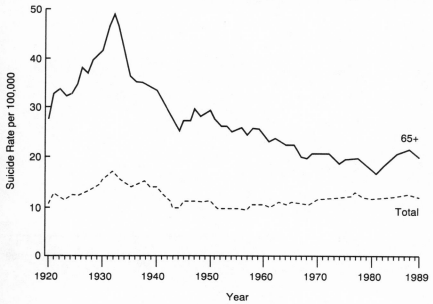

FIGURE 1–1

*Suicide Rates for the Total U.S. Population
and Those 65 and Older*

the elderly population as a whole does not appear to be closely associated with their decreased suicide rates, the increasing number of women compared to men in older age categories was significantly related to the decline. Women are a low-risk group for suicide at all ages (and especially in old age), while men are generally a high-risk group both overall and particularly in old age. As the total aged population came to include larger proportions of women after 1930, the effect was to contribute to the decrease in elderly suicide rates. In addition, most of the declines in elderly suicide were among males, and this also accelerated the decline over the influence that might be attributable to increasing numbers of females alone.

Another factor that influenced the decreasing suicide rates in old age is economic in nature. The economic status of individuals 65 and older improved greatly after 1930. The passage of the social security act in 1935 and the Older Americans Act and Medicare/Medicaid legislation in 1965 contributed greatly to the improved financial sta-

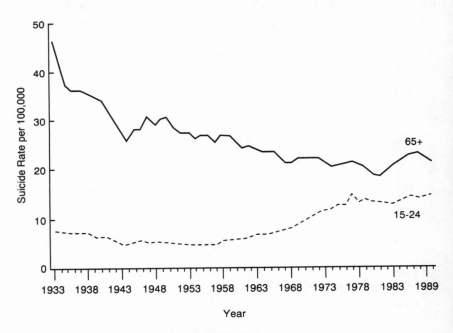

FIGURE 1–2

Suicide Rates for the Teenaged Population
and Those 65 and Older*

*Category includes young adults to age of 24.

tus of older people. Social programs and services for the elderly were greatly expanded and improved between 1935 and 1980, another key factor cited to explain the drop in the suicide rate during that period.

The improvement in techniques for diagnosing and treating depression, a major factor in later-life suicide, has been cited as another reason. The research conducted on depression and aging led to improved techniques for diagnosing depression, the discovery of antidepressant medications, and advances in electroconvulsive therapy.

Recently suicide researchers have turned their attention to the question of why the rate of elderly suicide has been steadily increasing since 1980. Although it is too early to draw solid conclusions, several explanations have been offered. Some suggest that the increase merely reflects the larger population of elders. Others believe that improved data collection and record keeping by coroners and medical examiners is responsible; that is, they claim that the rate has not increased but that society is more likely now to record and report suicides accurately. Neither of these explanations, however, focuses on changes in older adults or on societal conditions affecting older adults as important reasons for the rise.

TABLE 1–1

Suicide Rates, 1980–1989

Year	U.S. Population	Teenagers* (15–24)	Older Adults (65 and Older)
1980	11.82	12.3	17.65
1981	12.02	12.3	17.05
1982	12.18	12.1	18.31
1983	12.09	11.9	19.23
1984	12.30	12.5	20.00
1985	12.50	12.9	21.00
1986	12.80	13.2	21.60
1987	12.70	12.9	21.70
1988	12.40	13.2	20.90
1989	12.20	13.3	20.10

*Category includes young adults to age of 24.

Some students of the problem have related the increase in suicide rates to the changing conditions that older adults face and to various societal conditions affecting them. Experts argue that advances in medical technology may be partly responsible for the higher rate of suicide among the elderly. Advanced medical technology has greatly extended the quantity of physical life, possibly prolonging the period of time in which older people suffer from debilitating, painful health conditions. Many elderly may choose not to live so many years in poor physical health, in spite of the ability of medical technology to extend their physical lives. Many older adults are well aware of the problems associated with Alzheimer's disease and other debilitating illnesses and may fear living a long time if it means that they might develop such conditions.

The political and economic changes occurring in the 1980s are cited as well. Cutbacks in the food stamp program and in various social programs serving the elderly are considered important factors in increasing economic hardships and social isolation faced by many older adults. Threatened cutbacks in social security, Medicare, and Medicaid benefits may also be factors. Older adults are fearful of losing their money, dignity, and personal control. Faced with the constant fear of reduced social security benefits and payments made through Medicare and Medicaid and the fear of becoming a financial drain on the family, many may choose to end their lives.

Suicide increasingly is being accepted as a solution for life's problems, particularly the problems of older adults. Society has become more tolerant of suicide and even has actively endorsed it as a solution to some of the problems faced by our old. Arguments in favor of the "right to die," "death with dignity," and "rational suicide" have abounded recently. The Hemlock Society, an organization that advocates suicide as an acceptable solution to certain problems, has experienced dramatic growth since 1980. Political activists in California have taken steps to introduce legislation to legalize lethal injections for terminally ill individuals. Ethicists and scholars have argued convincingly for health care cost containment and health care rationing on the basis of age. The growing acceptance of suicide sends a powerful message to older adults who are already feeling lonely and isolated, unwanted, unneeded, and unloved: suicide is acceptable and possibly even desirable for someone their age in their predicament.

It's Worse Than Reported

An analysis of officially reported suicide rates indicates the significantly higher suicide rate of older adults. Dramatic as these figures are, they drastically underestimate the actual frequency of suicide among the elderly. They represent only officially recorded, reported suicides using overt methods such as guns, hanging, jumping, and wrist slashing and fail to take into account the many suicides that result from less obvious methods. Older adults who starve themselves to death or do not take their life-sustaining medications are not included in official suicide data, nor are those who intentionally mix drugs and alcohol or have fatal accidents that actually were intentional. Many deaths from suicide are never investigated and are reported mistakenly as accidents or deaths from natural causes, particularly when the victim is old.

Official suicide statistics reflect primarily the situation of older people who live outside institutions. Those living in nursing homes and other facilities are less likely to be included. Many residents of nursing homes, who are often too frail to engage in more overt suicidal acts or have limited access to more violent methods, engage in less overt suicidal acts. For example, individuals resorting to Intentional Life Threatening Behavior (ILTB) may refuse to eat, drink, take medications, or adhere to medical regimens. These less obvious forms of suicide lead to death just as surely as using a gun. They result in general debilitation, congestive heart failure, and other fatal conditions. The death certificate usually specifies the resultant physical illness as the cause of death rather than suicide. Failed suicide attempts can leave an older adult severely brain damaged, destroy the stomach, or cause other serious damage. Taking into account the untold number of deaths from this intentional life-threatening behavior and other less overt forms of suicide, the rate of suicide among those aged 65 and over may be twice as high as the officially reported rate.

Since 1980 there has been a dramatic increase in the number of reported double suicides or love-pact suicides, murder-suicides, and assisted suicides or "mercy" killings. In most of these incidents, at least one person is 65 or older. Ann Wickett, the former wife of Derek Humphry, founder of the Hemlock Society in California, recently became interested in what she calls "double exits." In her book by that title, she reports the results of her investigation. Between 1980 and 1987, ninety-seven documented cases occurred in which both spouses died together: thirty-one double suicides and sixty-six mercy killings/suicides. In the two previous decades, only a half-dozen such cases were reported. The rate of double suicides thus jumped to ten times what it had been in the three previous decades, and mercy killings/suicide jumped more than twenty times. These figures probably represent a drastic underreporting of the actual frequency of such deaths.

At-Risk Elders

Some older individuals are at greater risk of committing suicide than are others. Older men, for example, are much more likely to kill themselves than are older women. Older whites are at greater risk than are minority elders. The widowed are at increased risk. The "old old" (those age 75 and over) are at greater risk than the "young old" (ages 65 to 74). Nursing home residents are at risk, as are depressed or alcoholic elders.

Men Are More Vulnerable

At all stages of the life cycle, males are more likely to commit suicide than females and are three times more likely to die from suicide. In the oldest age category (age 85 and over), males are twelve times more likely to commit suicide than females. The suicide rate for males aged 65 and older is four times higher than the suicide rate for the nation as a whole. The rate increases linearly into the last decade of life, whereas the female rate peaks in midlife and then declines. White, widowed, older males are the most at risk of suicide.

Men are more vulnerable to suicide for several reasons. First, they are more likely than females to use violent, lethal methods, such as hanging, jumping, or shooting. In 1987, 67 percent of the males aged 65 and older in the United States used a gun, compared to only 30 percent of the females in the same age group. In some states, the number using guns is even greater. My recent study conducted in Virginia (Osgood, 1988) showed that over eight years, 87 percent of the males and 50 percent of the females aged 65 and over used guns to commit suicide. Males are more likely to be familiar with and comfortable with firearms; they may have been in the military or hunted in younger years. Males are also more likely than females to have access to guns. In our culture, guns are a symbol of masculinity. Females not only are less familiar with guns and have less access to them but do not choose shooting for aesthetic reasons; death by shooting is bloody and disfiguring. Females usually choose less violent methods, such as poisoning, pills, or suffocation.

Elderly males are more likely to suffer cumulative role loss—losing both the work role and often the role of spouse. Peter Townsend, a British gerontologist, calls that change or discontinuity in social engagements "desolation." It is experienced most acutely by male widowers, who have lost roles in work and family.

Race Makes a Difference

White elderly males are more likely to commit suicide than are minority males. For minority males, suicide rates peak in young adulthood; for whites, suicide rates peak in old age. Compared to black males and white females, aged white males in American society suffer the most severe loss of social status, power, and money. That loss represents one possible explanation for their dramatically higher rates of suicide. By comparison, women generally and minority males, two groups that traditionally have held lower status positions, have less to lose after retirement than do white males and thus tend to have lower rates of suicide than white males.

Minority males have more involvement in family, church, and other social relational systems. Elderly blacks are more likely to be wanted and needed in the family system, sometimes because of economic necessity but also because old age is respected by blacks, who feel that elders belong and are useful and productive. The intense support networks and strong human relationships that characterize the black community protect elderly blacks against suicide.

Elderly white males, particularly if they are widowed, tend to be isolated socially and emotionally. Unlike widows, widowed males are in the minority in late life and find few others in the same situation with whom they can talk. They are seldom seen in seniors' groups, local church activities, or other social events. Unlike older widows, they seldom form close, intimate emotional bonds with other males or females. Many elderly males live totally isolated, never seeing friends, neighbors, or family.

The current cohort of males is not likely to be comfortable cooking, cleaning, and taking care of the house. Widowed males, who find themselves in the traditional female domain, often eat poorly and feel they are useless. Minority males who lose their spouse are more likely to be members of an extended family system and do not face the extreme difficulties confronting white widowers.

Older Does Not Mean Safer

The old old—those aged 75 and over—represent an at-risk population, confirmed by their rate of suicide, which is much higher than those aged 65 to 74. The suicide rate for old-old males is more than 50 percent higher than the rate for females in that age group. Based on their study conducted in Arizona, Robert Kastenbaum and Richard Coppedge (1985) found such dramatically higher suicide rates among the old old compared to the young old that they referred to the situation among the old old as a countertrend—a reversal of the prevailing trend of decreasing suicide rates among the old. In the five-year study period, Kastenbaum and Coppedge found that the suicide rate for old-old males rose from 47.7 to 72.2 per 100,000, more than half again as high as a decade earlier. The rate for those aged 65 to 74 declined 10 percent during the same period. The researchers also noted an increase in the rate of suicide among old-old women, from 6.2 to 8.8 per 100,000.

In rural Arizona, the suicide rate for those aged 75 and older was extremely high, 88.8 per 100,000, reflecting the extreme social isolation of an individual in advanced years living in a sparsely populated place and unable to get out and about. The same is likely true for the old old in Wyoming, Montana, Alaska, and the other states with the highest rates of elderly suicide in the United States.

The old old are the most vulnerable to death from suicide because of their increased physical vulnerability and frailty. Engaging in any type of suicidal act, even a passive act such as starvation, has more devastating effects on the oldest individuals, who are depleted physically and have diminished recuperative powers. The old old are more likely to suffer medical complications from any suicide attempt that results in death. Physically and socially isolated from others, they are less likely to be discovered before it is too late. In many cases no family member, friend, or neighbor has regular contact with individuals of such advanced age. Consequently, there is no one to see drastic changes in mood or behavior or to hear hints before the individual makes a suicidal act.

Nursing Home Suicide

Residents of nursing homes and other long-term-care facilities, many of them aged 75 or older, are at increased risk of killing themselves. More than 23,000 long-term-care facilities serve over 1.5 million older adults, with the number of nursing home residences expected to increase more than 50 percent by 2020. Compared to older residents who live in the community, institutionalized elders are more likely to be older, physically frailer, cognitively impaired, and unmarried. They have suffered the loss of home and possessions, money, privacy, freedom, independence, and autonomy.

A recent national study of suicide in long-term-care facilities (Osgood, Brant & Lipman, 1990), which surveyed over a thousand such facilities across the country, revealed that suicide was reported and recorded in only 20 percent of the facilities studied. A more intensive and in-depth follow-up showed a drastic underreporting of the problem. More institutionalized older adults who died by suicide chose self-starvation and refusal to take life-sustaining medicines as their methods. As in the community population, those most at risk were white males and the old old. Most of these suicides were recorded not as suicides but as death from natural causes.

The Deadly Triangle

Psychological factors play a critical role in later-life suicide. Multiple losses and stresses—physical, emotional, mental, financial, and social—experienced by older adults contribute to depression and alcoholism, two precipitating factors in later-life suicide. The majority of older adults who take their own lives are suffering from depression. The National Institute on Alcohol Abuse and Alcoholism estimates that one-third of all suicides are alcoholics. The relationship between alcoholism and depression is strong. Many older individuals begin drinking to relieve their loneliness and psychological pain, although alcohol in fact is a depressant and contributes to rather than relieves depression. Depression, alcoholism, and suicide are a deadly triangle.

The Future Outlook

The "age wave" is coming, declared Dychtwald and Flower in their important book, *Age Wave* (1989). They identify three separate, unprecedented demographic phenomena converging to produce the coming age wave: the senior boom, the birth dearth, and the aging of the baby boom generation.

The senior boom results from the fact that Americans are living longer today than ever before in history. A child born in 1900 could expect to live approximately forty-five years; a child born today can expect to live approximately 76 years. Life expectancy at age 65 has also increased; in fact, it rose more between 1950 and 1980 than it had in the first half of the century. According to projections of the Census Bureau, life expectancy will reach 80 years by 2040. Life expectancy at age 65 in 1900 was 11.9 years; in 1980 it was 16 years. Thus, the average person today who has survived to 65 years can expect another 16 years of life (white males 13.7 years, white females 18.1, black males 13.8, black females 17.6). Today there are more long-lived people in our society, and in the rest of the world, than at any previous time in history.

Since 1900 the number and percentage of the population aged 65 and over has increased dramatically, from approximately 3 million (representing 4 percent of the total population) in 1900, to 12 million in 1950, to more than 30 million today (representing approximately 12 percent of the total population). In the last one hundred years, the population aged 65 and older has increased twelve times. The Census Bureau estimates that over 35 million Americans will be aged 65 or older in 2000 and more than 87 million by 2040.

The fastest-growing segment of the older population is the old-old group, and of these, the group aged 85 and older is increasing most rapidly. In 1900 fewer than 5,000 Americans were 85 or older; today over 3 million are in that age group. Estimates are that there will be close to 20 million people aged 85 and older by 2050.

Occurring at the same time as the senior boom is a birth dearth. Since 1900, Americans have been having fewer babies. Many baby boomers (those born between 1946 and 1964) are choosing not to have any children or to have only one child. In 1986, the fertility rate in the United States reached the lowest ever recorded in history.

The third phenomenon producing the coming age wave is the aging of the baby boom generation. Between 1946 and 1964, one-third of all Americans now living were born. By 2011, when the first baby boomers turn 65, there will be more than 52 million Americans aged 65 and older.

Many students of elderly suicide warn of a wave of suicides coming as the baby boomers enter old age, bringing with them the unique economic, social, and psychological problems of their generation—especially competition for jobs, mates, and other resources, as well as residual traumas of the Vietnam war experience. The recent steady rise in suicide rates may become even more dramatic in the next few decades. But even if there is no increase at all in the rate of elderly suicide, the numbers of elderly suicides may double and triple as the ranks of the elderly swell. If the rate of suicide for those aged 65 and older remains the same as it is now, by 2030 we can expect that nearly 13,000 older Americans may commit suicide annually—34 per day, one every 45 minutes.*

The fastest-growing segment of the U.S. population, those aged 85 and older, is also the group at highest risk for suicide. If the findings presented from Kastenbaum and Coppedge's study in Arizona are representative of many other states, we can expect an even larger rise in suicide rates for the old. Unless preventive measures are taken immediately, the specter of increasing suicides among the old will rise to epidemic proportions.

*The data related to the year 2030 are derived from figures presented by Dr. John McIntosh in the Shneidman Award Presentation at the annual meeting of the American Association of Suicidology in New Orleans in 1990. These data will be published in the journal *Suicide and Life-Threatening Behavior* in 1992.

2

Growing Old in the Society of the Young

Well, I thought it would be dramatic if there was an old man around while they were packing the pictures. A poor old man, trying to get a job helping them. But they can't use him—he's in the way—not even as cannon fodder. They want strong young people in the world. And it turns out he's the man who painted the pictures many years ago.

—F. Scott Fitzgerald, "A Man in the Way"

The poignant quotation from F. Scott Fitzgerald illustrates Americans' core attitude about old people. Elders are viewed as useless people whose lives are over.

In an attempt to discover what it is like to be old in America, a young industrial designer assumed the appearance and character of an 85-year-old woman. In 1979 Pat Moore, author of the book *Disguised,* began a three-year journey into the world of the old in America. With the help of a makeup artist, Moore learned to apply heavy prosthetic makeup to add decades to her 26-year-old face. She bought jowls, crow's-feet, under-eye bags, and extra neck skin. A white wig covered her hair. To complete the look, she wore a pair of heavy orthopedic shoes, used white gloves to hide her young hands, walked with a cane, wore a pair of spectacles to hide her youthful eyes, and stained and discolored her youthful white teeth with a special crayon. She wore inexpensive, extra-large housedresses purchased at the local dime store and a shawl. To feel like an old woman, she put baby oil in her eyes to blur her vision, taped her fingers to simulate the effect of arthritis, put small splints of balsa wood behind each knee to restrict movement, and used a body wrap to create a humped-over look. Her disguise was complete.

As she wandered disguised through city streets all over the United States, Moore was routinely ignored, treated rudely and crudely, and nearly beaten to death. Many people totally ignored her as if she did not exist. Others assumed she was hard of hearing and shouted at her or pushed in front of her to get on a bus or to get ahead in the grocery line. She was intentionally short-changed when buying items at the store, an easy trick because one-dollar and ten-dollar bills look and feel the same to those with dimmed vision. Worst of all, some teenagers took pleasure in bashing her.

Some of the incidents related in *Disguised* illustrate how we feel about and treat old people. On her first day in character, Moore boarded an airplane and was seated next to a gentleman who was about 60. The man totally ignored her; he did not respond to her attempts to interact with him as he buried his nose in a newspaper and totally avoided all eye contact and physical contact in spite of the fact that he was seated beside her. The incident left her feeling as if she wore a visible label, "OLD."

Walking along the streets, she was shoved, bumped, and nearly run over by passers-by many times. She was hurt physically and also emotionally hurt to think that she was viewed as so useless and worthless that people did not feel the need even to acknowledge the incident, let alone inquire if she were hurt or apologize.

She experienced particularly bad treatment in stores and shops. Younger customers pushed in front of her, and clerks treated her rudely and unfairly. One day she went into a stationery store to buy a typewriter ribbon. The clerk was impatient, rude, and uncaring. He as much as called her stupid when she could not remember the type of ribbon she needed and did not look at her when he gave her change. Giving the gentleman the benefit of the doubt and not assuming her ill treatment was necessarily due to her age, Moore went to the same store the next day but this time not in character. Although she wore the same dress, said the same things, and acted in exactly the same manner as she had the day before, the transaction was totally different. The same clerk was cheerful and helpful, eager to help a young women. He laughed it off when she said she forgot the type of ribbon she needed and was helpful in finding the correct one. He was friendly as he counted out her exact change for her.

Of all the incidents she experienced as the old Pat Moore, the most significant and most brutal occurred late one night in Harlem. She had stayed out later than she intended. She was trying to hurry to the bus stop, but in her body wrap and heavy orthopedic shoes, with balsa wood behind each knee, it was hard to move fast. Before she could reach her bus stop, she was attacked from behind by teenaged boys, who grabbed her and threw her down. They took her purse and then danced around her, jeering and taunting, kicking her repeatedly in the neck and stomach. Her knees were broken, and she was badly bruised all over her torso, legs, and arms. The nerves in her left hand were permanently damaged, and she will always have to wear a splint and a brace on her left hand and wrist. As she was being beaten, she knew the vulnerability of being old—helpless, physically frail, unable to fight back, powerless, and at the mercy of the younger, stronger, ruthless teenagers.

Moore's social experiment dramatically illustrates the ageism that exists in our society. Ageism, a term coined by Robert Butler in 1968, is similar to racism and sexism. He defined ageism as "a deep and profound prejudice against the elderly and a systematic stereotyping of and discrimination against people because they are old." In other words, ageism means "not wanting to have all those old people around." It results in a deep hatred of and aversion toward people who are old simply because they are old. Like racism and sexism, ageism is a form of prejudice and discrimination against one group in the society—in this case, the old.

The Roots of Ageism in America

The United States has not always been an ageist society. In colonial days, when reaching old age was rare, old age was venerated. Until the late 1700s the old held all major positions of power and authority in the family, church, and state. In an agrarian-based economy, the old, who owned the land, were also in positions of economic power.

Once We Weren't Ageist

In his insightful book, *Growing Old in America,* David Fischer (1977) describes the position of the elderly in colonial days. In the 1600s and most of the 1700s, the old were exalted, obeyed, respected, and honored; old age conveyed a coveted status. Elders ruled local churches, and most prestigious seats in the meetinghouse were reserved for them. Elders held these tenures for life. The elderly were honored at special ceremonial occasions. In New England and the southern colonies, the principle of eldership, or rule by elders, was observed in state government, where elders held positions of political power. John Winthrop, Roger Williams, and William Byrd are examples of leaders who translated the prestige of more than 70 years of age into political power. Somewhat later Ben Franklin and other elder statesmen were important leaders of the new nation.

Elders were honored and respected in the family and retained their positions as the head of household into their later years. They were allowed to speak first, were offered seats by younger people, and were allowed to walk in front of younger people.

The honor of elders was rooted in religious ideology based on the Scriptures. The Puritans and Calvinists viewed long life as a sign that an individual had found favor with God. During the seventeenth century, Jesus and the angels were pictured as old. The commandment to honor father and mother dictated honor and respect for older family members. The Puritans, who pictured God as a very old man with a long white beard, believed that there was "something of the image of God in age" (Mather, 1716). The dominant Judeo-Christian ethic was the basis of veneration of the old during that time.

The power and position of the old in colonial days was rooted in financial reality. Older people owned the land and retained legal and financial control until they died and their sons inherited their land. Sons had solid financial reasons for respecting and honoring their parents in order to receive their inheritance.

It was common for individuals to exaggerate their age and to dress in ways that made them appear older. For example, they wore white powdered wigs, and the fashions of the time flattered age and were designed to make one appear older.

Respect for Elders Erodes

Between 1780 and 1820, when the French and American Revolutions occurred, attitudes toward the old began to change, a change that has continued to the present. The framers of the Declaration of Independence advocated equality and liberty for all. The idea of equality destroyed the traditional system in which an age hierarchy gave older people preferential treatment. The system of relations based on a hierarchy of age came to represent the old order, which had to be replaced if the new ideals of equality and liberty were to be achieved.

These ideological changes had a profound effect on the nature of age relations and the cultural value system in America. The emphasis on freedom and equality resulted in an individual achievement orientation, which has dominated our society for the last 150 years. It places a high value on activity, personal productivity through work, materialism, success, individual achievement, independence, and self-sufficiency. Older adults who are no longer able to produce due to physical and mental changes or to social policies that remove them from gainful employment (such as retirement) are at a distinct disadvantage in a society dominated by such a value orientation.

In the mid-eighteenth century, the signs of change emerged. The practice of seating elders in the most honored places in the meeting-house was discontinued in some New England towns. Fashions instead flattered a younger figure. Wigs were replaced by hairpieces that made men look younger. As society became more secularized, the power of religion weakened. Laws regarding inheritance of property changed so that the eldest son lost his automatic inheritance rights.

Ageism, which began to develop in the early 1800s, is deeply rooted in the sociocultural structure of American society. In the 1800s many social changes took place that resulted in a decreased status of the old: changes in urbanization and technology, family relationships, mobility patterns, demographic shifts, and in the structure and organization of work.

As the nation became urbanized and industrialized, young people began to move away from the family farm to seek their fortunes working in factories in the cities. These shifting mobility patterns weakened kinship ties as the large extended family system was replaced by smaller nuclear families comprising husband, wife, and children. Older people were left behind on farms and in rural areas, and interaction between family members in the older and younger generations was reduced. Adult children were no longer dependent on their parents and grandparents for economic survival and inherited land.

As the pace of technological and industrial change quickened, older people found themselves in a poorer position. Their knowledge and skills rapidly became obsolete. Farming, crafts, and other skills that took a lifetime to learn were no longer valued in a fast-paced, technologically sophisticated culture dominated by machines. The emphasis on individual achievement was strong during the industrialization period that peaked in 1890. Human effort was seen as the key to progress.

A new type of work organization, the bureaucracy, arose. A bureaucracy is characterized by a highly specialized division of labor, formal rules, impersonal procedures, hierarchical chains of command, and centralized authority. Competition increases, and workers are expected to produce at a certain level. Older adults were at a distinct disadvantage in such a system.

Demographics had a major impact on how we view and treat older people today. In 1810 the median age in America began to rise, resulting in larger numbers of people over age 50 in the population. Since the mid-1800s the number of older people in the U.S. population and the average life expectancy have increased greatly. As more people live longer, intergenerational competition for jobs and economic resources increases. Perceived economic scarcity is a factor in ageism.

The passage of the Social Security Act in 1935 was one way to remove a large segment of the working-age population out of the job market, and the trend toward retirement quickened in the competition for jobs after World War II. The implementation of retirement from paid, productive work was a major factor contributing to ageism. Retirement at age 65 signaled a loss of productivity, money, success, achievement, and self-sufficiency. Older adults no longer in the work force were viewed as nonproductive, dependent, worthless, and useless in a society that so highly valued individual achievement. In his classic study of American society, Robin Williams (1970) concluded that occupational success is more than a life goal in American society; it is the outstanding trait of American culture.

Today many proponents of health care cost containment, health care rationing, and euthanasia are concerned with the use of scarce economic and health care resources by the increasing number of long-lived people. Older people are viewed as a social and economic burden to be borne by younger, more productive members of society. Older people as a group are seen as "people about to die."

In addition to being ruled by an achievement orientation, America is also a country in which youth and beauty are highly valued. The glorification of youth and development of the youth cult in America began in the nineteenth century and grew rapidly in the twentieth, and it now flourishes in our present atmosphere of narcissism. Youth is associated with vitality, activity, and freshness. To be young is to be fully alive, exciting, attractive, healthy, and vigorous. Old age, on the other hand, is associated with decline, disease, disability, and death rather than wisdom, inner peace, and other positive qualities.

"Whom the Gods Love Die Young"

Our ideas about age are also inherited from the classical Greeks, who viewed aging as an unmitigated misfortune and terrible tragedy. The Greeks believed "those whom the gods love die young." Youth was the only period of life of true happiness. During the heroic age, manhood was measured by the standard of physical prowess. Old age robbed the person of such prowess and the ability to fight like a valiant warrior and robbed males of sexual powers.

Early Greek and Roman writings were filled with images glorifying youth and beauty and denigrating old age, which was associated with the loss of youth and beauty. *Oedipus Rex,* written in the middle of the fifth century, depicted old age as a time of decline in physical and mental functioning. This view is expressed well in the words of Mimnermus, an ancient Greek writer: "The fruit of youth rots early; it barely lasts as long as the light of day. And once it is over, life is worse than death" (quoted in Chinen, 1989, pp. 4–5). A similar view is expressed by the Roman writer, Ovid, who vividly described the losses, frustrations, and sadness of old age.

The Roman poet Juvenal wrote one of the most scathing descriptions of old age and its effect on male sexuality:

A long old age is full of continual evils;
Look, first of all, at the face, unshapely, foul, and disgusting,
Unlike its former self, a hide, not a skin, and chopfallen;
Look at the wrinkles too, like those which a mother baboon
Carves on her face in the dark shade of Numidian jungles.
Young people vary a lot; one, you will find, is more handsome,
One more robust, but the old are all alike, and they look it—
Doddering voices and limbs, bald heads, running noses, like
   children's,

Munching their bread, poor old things, with gums that are utterly
  toothless,
Such a disgusting sight to themselves, their wives, and their children.
They are even despised by Cossus the legacy-hunter.
Wine is no good anymore, food everlasting tasteless.
As for the act of love, that long ago was forgotten,
Or if you should try, though you play with it all night long,
You will never rise, you cannot, to meet the occasion.
This is a state of things to pray for, this impotent sickness?
When desire outruns performance, who can be happy?
                                        (Humphries, 1958, pp. 128–129)

The image of the strong, young man also dominated Greek art and sculpture from the fifth through seventh centuries B.C. The love of youth is evident in the statues of young men and women of the Archaic period, the Parthenon frieze, and the well-known statue of the discus thrower that accentuates the strong, young, muscular physique of an athlete at the peak of his physical powers. Except in the Hellenistic period (323–27 B.C.), Greek sculptors never portrayed older figures.

So ingrained was classical ageism in Western thought that Ponce de Leon, the Spanish explorer, set out on a voyage more than 400 years ago to discover the fountain of youth, a spring whose waters had the power to restore youth. Today his quest for youth continues. A society in which many people highly prize speed, progress, productivity, and individual achievement has little use for the old, who represent dependency and decrepitude.

Why We're Afraid of the Old

Psychological factors influence ageism in our culture. The youth cult grows out of a profound fear of growing old. Through the ages, few fears have cut as deeply into the human soul as the fear of aging. Americans especially have a stark terror of growing old. Old age is associated with loss of independence, physical disease, mental decline, loss of youthful vitality and beauty, and finally death, and old people are reminders of our own mortality. Because many people have limited contact with healthy, vibrant old people and lack accurate knowledge about the aging process, their fears escalates.

Gerontophobia, the unrealistic fear of aging and old people, is at the root of ageism in American society. Young people seek to avoid old people in an attempt to deny the inevitability of aging and death. Their avoidance serves as a psychological defense mechanism. Young people do not want to lose their independence, their power and status in the work world, and the beauty and vitality of youth. They do not want to experience physical pain and sickness and, most of all, do not want to die. The feeling, unrealistic as it may seem, is that if we can close our eyes to old age, it will go away, and we will remain perpetually young. As Jonathan Swift observed centuries ago, "Everyman desires to live long, but no man would be old."

Some Societies Still Honor Age

In a number of societies, however, the old are still honored and respected.

Historically, in many primitive societies of the world, the old were highly honored, at least until the very end of life when they became mentally or physically decrepit. In his analysis of seventy-one countries in the 1940s, Leo Simmons reported that in many primitive societies, which were simple rural societies, the old held the most honored positions. The chiefs, shamans and religious leaders, and major owners of land and animals were old. The eldest member of the extended family held the position of greatest honor, and his authority and opinions were highly respected by all younger family members. Special food and drinks were reserved for the oldest members, and certain magical and spiritual rituals could be conducted only by the very old. The elderly were well cared for by younger family members and other young people in the tribe or village.

In these small, tradition-oriented agrarian societies with limited technology, the old were viewed as the wisest members. They possessed knowledge, wisdom, and experience. They knew how to cure physical ills, how to plant and grow food, the best places and the best ways to hunt game, and the best ways to please the gods and to perform magic. In such societies where the written word is not developed, the only means of transmitting knowledge is through oral tradition. The old were a rich repository of tales, stories, cultural folklore, and legends. For these reasons, the aged were sought out for their vast knowledge and were in great demand at family gatherings and community ceremonies as storytellers, instructors in dancing and games, and public narrators of past events.

Old age is still highly respected in some cultures. In the Middle East, for example, old age is viewed as the summit of life. Based on his study of the Kirghiz of Afghanistan, Nazif Shahrani (1981) concluded that the old are in major positions of power and status in the family and in the community. They are provided with economic security and given respect by younger members of the family and community for their knowledge and skills. Old people play a major role in the rearing and socialization of grandchildren and are seldom isolated from the family. Young people wait on and help them, and they are given the most comfortable and most honored seat in the homes of younger people. The old occupy the most favored positions in public gatherings, are served first, and are given the best portions of food. Younger people are expected to be quiet and attentive when old people are speaking. Growing old in this culture is viewed as a process of growing wise and gaining respect and authority. Old age is cherished as a triumph in life.

Even in some modernized, urbanized, technologically sophisticated societies, the old still are respected and honored. Influenced by the Eastern traditions of filial piety and respect for age, which is also apparent in China and Korea, Japan represents the best modern-day example of respect and honor for elders. The son of missionaries who lived in Japan, gerontologist Erdman Palmore (1975) has presented an elaborate description of age relations in Japan.

In Japan the term used for the aged is *otoshiyon,* which means "honorable age achieved." Indeed, many of the terms in the Japanese language referring to the old are honorific. Although the veneration of elders that characterized traditional Japanese society has lessened since World War II, older people in Japan still receive deference, honor, and respect. They hold positions of authority and honor in the family and are considered senior advisers on family problems. Older Japanese in rural areas still play a major role in farming and fishing, and those who are artists and professors in urban areas are respected as national treasures. Many Japanese consider it a matter of national pride to continue working and contributing to their family, community, and country.

In Japan older people generally hold higher society positions than young people and thus command respect and deference. Japan is still dominated by the Confucian value of filial piety, which specifies the obligations of children and grandchildren to their parents and grand-parents. Over half of all Japanese elders live with their children. In earlier times ancestor worship was practiced regularly in Japan, and vestiges still exist. The old represent those who will soon be one's dead ancestors.

Unlike the United States, Japanese society is not characterized by individual achievement and independence. Rather, it values the social group; dependence on and loyalty to the group is paramount. To function well and to prosper as a group, all ages, including the old, must be respected and integrated into our society.

Elders in Japan are treated with kindness and respect by the national government. In 1963 the National Law for the Welfare of Elders was passed, legally requiring love and respect for elders and protection of their welfare. Respect for Elders' Day, begun in 1963, is a dramatic national expression of love and respect for elders. In 1973 the Central Line of the Japanese Railways, which serves Tokyo and its western suburbs, reserved certain prime seats on the bus for elders. Although that law is obeyed more in rural areas than in the city, Palmore concluded that "the theory of marked decline in the status of the aged as a necessary result of industrialization is false. On the contrary, Japan shows that a tradition of respect for the aged can maintain their relatively high status and integration despite industrialization" (p. 128).

Even within the United States, at least one cultural group honors and respects the old, the Old Order Amish, the most conservative followers of Jacob Ammann, a seventeenth-century Swiss Anabaptist who founded that faction within the Swiss Mennonite group in 1893 and who have settled in eastern Pennsylvania, Ohio, New York, Delaware, Maryland, Illinois, and Indiana.

Old Order Amish are characterized by strong religious beliefs that require rejection of modern technologies and separation from the worldly values of the larger society. They are thus mainly farmers who live and work on family farms. The Amish consider the family the most important social institution. They live in extended families, with as many as four generations living on the same property; the aging live with and are taken care of by their children and grandchildren until their death. The eldest male members serve as consultants, giving important advice on family members and the running of the family farm, and grandmothers have a major role in the running of the family household (Brubaker and Michael, 1987).

Older Amish men retain positions of authority in the community's religious life, serving as bishops, ministers, and deacons. They are respected for their interpretation of Scripture, on which their favored position in the culture is based.

Myths and Stereotypes about Aging and the Old

Ageism is manifested through stereotypes and myths about old people and aging. Stereotypes are generalized opinions or beliefs produced by irrational thinking that serves to categorize people so that the world seems structured, ordered, and under control. By stereotyping, or classifying all people who share a particular characteristic such as their age, there is a danger that a few characteristics will be overemphasized, while other equally important characteristics will be ignored. Stereotypes are usually negative and produce negative feelings and emotions such as hatred or fear.

Euphemisms about and stereotypes of old people and later years abound. We speak of the "golden years" and "golden agers" and talk about "growing old gracefully." In medical circles old patients are stereotyped as "crocks" or "vegetables." Other common terms for older people are *old fuddy duddy, little old lady,* and *dirty old man.* Old people are thought of as being fit for little else but sitting idly in a rocking chair. Older women are referred to as *old witch, old bag,* and *old biddy.* Old men are stereotyped as *old geezers, old goats,* and *old codgers.* Common stereotypes of aging view the old as out to pasture, over the hill, and all washed up.

Many myths about old people and the aging process also exist.

MYTH 1: After 65 everyone goes steadily downhill.

This myth implies physical and mental decline with age. Aging is thus associated with physical disease and decrepitude, mental decline, disability, and death. The fact is that age 65 is not a magical marker indicating the beginning of a downhill slope. Many 65 year olds are active and vigorous, in excellent physical health, and contributing to society. Many people remain young at age 70 or 80—and some are old at age 40 or 50.

MYTH 2: *Old people are senile or feebleminded.*

The senility myth portrays older people as disoriented, demented, feebleminded, and suffering from defective memory. The fact is that less than 5 percent of those age 65 and older suffers from some form of incurable, irreversible organic brain syndrome. Much of what passes as senility may in reality be the result of physical disease, depression, alcoholism, poor diet, or an adverse reaction to a particular medication.

MYTH 3: *Old people enter a second childhood.*

The infantilization of the old—seeing and treating them as children—is common in our society. Terms such as *honey, dearie,* and *sweetie* are reserved for children and old people. In some restaurants the "kiddies'" menu is for those under age 12 and over age 65. The myth suggests that old people are like children; they are dependent and need to be taken care of, lack full control over bowel and bladder functions, drool and dribble their food, and do not make a valuable contribution to society. In fact, unless they are suffering from a serious, debilitating physical disease or an organic brain syndrome, older people are fully functioning adults, capable of making their own decisions, handling their own financial and legal affairs, and meeting most of the challenges of daily living without assistance.

MYTH 4: *Old people are sexless and unattractive.*

According to the myth of sexual decline in later life, the old, and particularly women, are ugly and totally unappealing sexually. This myth also equates aging with lack of interest in and inability to perform the sexual act. However, research by Masters and Johnson (1966) and Hite (1976) has confirmed that the interest in and capacity for sexual relations continues into the 70s, 80s, and 90s for men and women. The decline in interest in or capability for sexual performance is not a result of the aging process; rather, it is related to physical illness, depression, alcoholism, and reaction to some medications.

MYTH 5: *Old people are cranky and grumpy.*

Old people are perceived as cranky, grumpy, grouchy, and difficult to get along with. Certainly it is true that sick old people are sometimes grumpy and cranky; but it is equally true that sick young people are cranky and grumpy and difficult to get alone with. Healthy elders are not necessarily grumpy or cranky. Some are and always have been unpleasant; others are cheerful and happy, easy going and friendly, and a real joy to be around—and they were probably like that when they were younger. An individual's age is no predictor of his or her temperament.

MYTH 6: *Old people are old-fashioned, conservative, and set in their ways.*

This myth portrays old people as backward, behind the times, old fogies, with old-fashioned ideas who are set in their ways and unable to change. Certainly many older adults become more stable in their attitudes; however, they continue to change as they perceive a need and to adapt to new life events, such as retirement, widowhood, and loss of their children. To survive the aging process, older adults have to adapt constantly to the changes and challenges that aging brings.

MYTH 7: *Old people have difficulty learning.*

The common saying, "You can't teach an old dog new tricks," espouses the myth that old people cannot learn anything new. Members of the larger society, particularly employers, view older people as slow workers with obsolete skills who are unable to learn new procedures and work habits. Employers often feel that investing in training of older workers is a waste of time and resources. The fact is that older adults can learn just as effectively as younger people. Studies show that it may take them longer, but they can learn. In terms of job performance, older workers are the most capable and most loyal employees. Compared to younger workers, they have fewer accidents and less absenteeism and remain longer with a company. Some may be slower at their job, but most perform steadily, consistently, and reliably, completing the same amount of work as the young over time.

MYTH 8: *Older people are nonproductive.*

In our fast-paced, technologically sophisticated country where the emphasis is on productivity, the myth of the old as nonproductive is prevalent. Older people are viewed as washed up and out to pasture, with nothing to contribute to society. Their knowledge and skills are devalued, and they are seen as useless and, worse, a burden to be borne by the younger members of society. To debunk this myth, we need only to think of the many productive older adults who have made significant contributions in the fields of music, art, science, peace, and politics in their later years: Arthur Rubinstein, Eubie Blake, Arthur Fiedler, Grandma Moses, George Burns, Thomas Edison, Albert Einstein, Frank Lloyd Wright, Linus Pauling, Claude Pepper, Henry Kissinger, and Ronald Reagan, among many others.

MYTH 9: *Old people are all alike.*

The myth of homogeneity portrays older people as all alike, with the same beliefs and values, identical needs and concerns. By this stereotype, we ignore old people as unique human beings. The fact is that of all the age groups, the old are the least alike. Babies and young children are pretty much alike. But old people have lived long, each experiencing a different world, interacting with different people, and dealing with many of life's problems. Today's generation of old people in America comprises largely immigrants from different countries, each with a unique culture. Some old people are rich; some poor. Some are conservative morally and politically; others liberal. Some are happy and cheerful; others sad and unhappy.

MYTH 10: *Old people live in a peaceful, serene world.*

This myth promotes the idea that older people have no problems, no stresses, and smooth sailing. The fact is that older people experience more problems, losses, and stresses than younger people. Many must learn to cope with unaccustomed amounts of leisure time after retirement. Many face the death of spouse, siblings, friends, and pets and must deal with grief. Others experience devastating changes in vision, hearing, and mobility. Life in the later years is anything but serene.

MYTH 11: Tomorrow's old people will be just like today's.

Those who accept this common belief that the next generation of older people will be just like the present cohort mistakenly assume that future generations of elders will have the same financial, social, and educational needs as the current generation. The fact is that future generations of older adults will be better educated and have higher expectations than the present generation. When the baby boomers become old, they will share a unique history, different from the present generation of older adults.

Sources of Ageism

In American culture, several mechanisms perpetuate and communicate ageist images, stereotypes, and myths: common aphorisms, literature, the media, and humor.

Aphorisms

Aphorisms about aging and older people permeate American culture. Some of the most common include: "You're not getting older, you're getting better"; "You can't trust anyone over 40"; "You're only as old as you feel"; and "Age before beauty." These common sayings convey the idea that age is something to be denied or feared and allude to imagined losses accompanying the aging process.

Negative Images through Words

The Western heritage in literature is replete with negative images of old age, beginning with medieval works. The foolish lust of older women is described in the works of Chaucer and Boccaccio. The physical ugliness and disgusting behavior of the old were frequently highlighted in fairy tales. The glorification of youth and denigration of age was a major literary theme in the Elizabethan period. Shakespeare despised old age. These sixteenth-century lines are attributed by some to Shakespeare:

> Crabbed age and youth cannot live together;
> Youth is full of pleasance, age is full of care;
> Youth like summer morn, age like winter weather;
> Youth like summer brave, age like winter bare;
> Youth is full of sport, age's breath is short;
> Youth is nimble, age is lame;
> Youth is hot and bold, age is weak and cold;
> Youth is wild, and age is tame.
> Age, I do abhor thee; youth, I do adore thee;
> O, my love, my love is young!
> Age, I do defy thee; O, sweet shepherd, hie thee,
> For methinks thou stay'st too long.

(The Passionate Pilgrim)

Jonathan Swift elaborated the same theme as the myth of Tithonos in his description of the Struldbrugs in *Gulliver's Travels*. In his world travels, Gulliver discovers a society in which some individuals are immortal. The Struldbrugs, as they are called by other members of their society, are "opinionated, peevish, covetous, morose, incapable of friendship, and dead to all natural affection." These immortals, forced to live most of their lives as old, decrepit people, have lost their teeth and hair, cannot taste their food, suffer many diseases, forget the names of common things, and even forget the people who were their dearest friends and relations. They are the most miserable of all creatures, without love or satisfaction.

More recently in American literature, the pathos and emptiness of old age are prominent themes. Ralph Waldo Emerson (1886) wrote the following about old age:

> Nature lends herself to these illusions, and adds dim sight, deafness, cracked voice, snowy hair, short memory and sleep. These also are masks, and all is not age that wears them. Nature is full of freaks, and now puts an old head on young shoulders, and then a young heart beating under four score winters. Youth is everywhere in place. Age, like woman, requires fit surroundings. Age is comely in coaches, in churches, in chairs of state and ceremony, in council-chambers, in courts of justice and historical societies. Age is becoming in the country.

A classical example of the pathos of old age is the dying old man portrayed by John Steinbeck in *The Grapes of Wrath* (1939). The old man, who remains nameless, has no personality. He is a bag of bones—wasting away, totally helpless, and totally dependent. In one of the final scenes in the book, and one of the most powerful in American literature, a young mother with a newborn infant breast-feeds the dying old man. The passage conveys him as helpless and dependent as a newborn baby. But it also portrays the profound generosity on the part of the young woman and the deep gratitude of the old man, a poignant illustration of intergenerational relations.

In the novel *To Be a Pilgrim* (1942), Joyce Cary describes old age in these words:

> Love is a delusion to the old, for who can love an old man? He is a nuisance; he has no place in the world. The old are surrounded by treachery for no one tells them truth. Either it is thought necessary to deceive them, for their own good, or nobody can take the trouble to give explanation or understanding to those who will carry both so soon into a grave. They must not complain of what is inevitable; they must not think evil. It is unjust to blame the rock for its hardness, the stream for its inconstancy and its flight, the young for the strength and the jewel brightness of their passage. An old man's loneliness is nobody's fault. He is like an old-fashioned hat which seems absurd and incomprehensible to the young, who never admired and wore such a hat.

The emptiness of old age is a major theme in American literature. In the poem "Gerontion" (1920), T. S. Eliot provides a description of the empty misery of an old man, "a dry brain in a dry season." In his works Eliot describes old age as an empty wasteland.

The negative images of aging and old age fill children's literature as well. In fact, there is a lack of older characters in children's books. And when they are in these books, especially in fairy tales, they are often portrayed as quiet and passive or cruel and scary figures. The witch in "Hansel and Gretel" and the witch in "Sleeping Beauty" are mean and frightening—and old. In "Snow White and the Seven Dwarfs," the wicked queen is an older woman, as is the wicked step-mother in "Cinderella." The old woman who lived in the shoe starves and spanks her children.

Old men are often portrayed as mean-spirited wizards with magical powers. Rumplestiltskin is the epitome of a hateful old man. In the "Three Billy Goats Gruff," the wicked trolls are old men with wrinkled skin and long beards.

Children are thus exposed very early to negative images of aging. These fairy tales are a major mechanism of the cultural transmission of ageist images, myths, and stereotypes. Happily, however, recent children's literature has begun to dispel these negative images.

Media Messages: Old Is Bad

The mass media in America have been described as "the cultural arm of American industry" (Gerbner, 1961). They are influenced by cultural stereotypes and by younger members of society, who control the major socioeconomic resources. Media images of old people and of aging are controlled by younger people, who devalue the old and dread growing old themselves. It is no surprise that the Madison Avenue image of aging and the old is less unflattering. There is a noticeable lack of older characters in television shows, on the radio, and in films. Although nearly 15 percent of the U.S. population is aged 65 or older, less than 5 percent of all television actors are in that age group. This omission of older characters gives the message that older people are not important in American society.

When older people do appear in television shows, they are usually cast in negative roles. Older males are much more likely than younger men to be portrayed as "bad guys." Older women are more likely than younger women to be cast as failures and to be treated rudely and disrespectfully. They seldom play glamorous and sexy roles. More often they are victims. Older black females particularly are often cast only to be killed or to serve as maids. Young and middle-aged men most often hold the powerful and exciting roles—with jobs, success, power, and money.

Aunt Blabby, a character of comedian Johnny Carson, is a composite of several negative stereotyped images of older women. Dressed in frumpy, outdated clothes, with her incessant talking, she is the stereotypical image of a silly old woman. Even the more positive image portrayed by the calm, easy-going, kind, concerned Marcus Welby, M.D., is a stereotype. Dr. Welby never has exciting adventures and does not appear to be a strong and vital man. He is the picture of the sweet old grandfather. The women on the "Golden

Girls," a currently popular television show, are also stereotypes of older women; they are ditzy, meddlesome busybodies and sex-starved females who cannot get a man.

Older characters on television often speak in creaky, high-pitched voices, wear ill-fitting and outdated clothes, use outdated slang, and are hard of hearing and a little senile. Fred Sanford ("Sanford and Son") represents the crotchety old man; Mother Jefferson ("The Jeffersons") is the picture of the nosy old woman. There are some positive portrays of older characters on television. Two examples are Angela Lansbury on "Murder, She Wrote" and Inspector Morse on the PBS Mystery series.

The most blatant negative stereotyping of older people appears in advertisements that stimulate consumer demand by exploiting the fear of aging. Commercial advertising in magazines and newspapers and on television and radio plays on fears of loss of youth, vitality, and appearance to promote new products. People are enticed to buy diet pills to lose weight, cream to cover wrinkles, hair dyes to cover the gray, elixirs to feel young and vigorous, and health spa memberships to keep youthful figures. All of these products promise consumers that they can cover up or hide the visible signs of aging. Advertisers offer hair conditioners and shampoos that ostensibly help us keep full heads of hair, toothpastes to give sex appeal, hand creams that make it hard to tell the mother's hands from her daughter's, and face oils and creams that promise to keep faces looking and feeling young and beautiful—forever. Advertisements promote youth and beauty and encourage people to see aging as something ugly, to be denied and covered up.

Other advertisements teach us that aging is painful and bothersome. Old people are featured in advertisements of pain medications to relieve nagging headaches and backaches, denture cream to keep dentures in place, laxatives to combat constipation, and pads because of incontinence.

Did You Hear the One About . . . ?

In every culture humor conveys attitudes about the aged. In our own society these attitudes are expressed through jokes, cartoons and comic strips, and birthday cards. Predominant themes include the decline of physical appearance, lessening of sexual ability, decline in mental and physical abilities, loss of attractiveness, and denial of aging. Humor about older women is more negative than humor about older men. The following ageist jokes are examples.

Two women met in a supermarket. One looked at the health food section and said, "I think I'll go on a health food diet." "Not me," replied the other. "At my age I need all the preservatives I can get."

On one occasion two widows were talking. One asked the other, "Have you ever seen a man that you liked?" The other replied, "My dear I'm with four men every day: I get up with Charlie Horse, I eat with Art Ritis, all day I live with Will Power, and at night I go to bed with Ben Gay!"

A woman was asked if she carried a memento of someone in her locket. "Yes, it's a lock of my husband's hair," she replied. "But your husband is still here," she was told. "Yes, but his hair isn't."

Three stages of male sexual development:
Young . . . . Tri-Weekly
Middle-Aged . . . . . Try Weekly
Old . . . . Try Weakly

How to Know You're Growing Older

Everything hurts, and what doesn't hurt doesn't work.

Your little black book contains only names ending in M.D.

You're still chasing women but can't remember why.

You sit in a rocking chair and can't get it going.

Your knees buckle and your belt won't.

Your back goes out more than you do.

You sink your teeth into a steak and they stay there.

Your pacemaker makes the garage door go up when you watch a pretty girl go by.

Cartoons and comic strips contain ageist images, as the examples here show.

"These pills should help your amnesia...
if memory serves."

"Grandma, do wrinkles hurt?"

Birthday cards offer numerous negative images of aging and the aged. Hallmark recently introduced an Over the Hill line of birthday cards, which reinforce many negative images of aging and the aged. One card in this line has the following caption on the front: "Don't Worry! Some Men Prefer Older Women." Inside the card reads: "Some Near-Senile, Stooped-over Ragged Men Who Talk to Waste-baskets, That Is. Happy Birthday." This line of products also features black wrapping paper, black crepe paper, and black balloons for birthday parties honoring those aged 40 and over.

Other examples of ageist cards include the following:

COVER: A frumpy old woman in tennis shoes and an old
    hat looking into a mirror with the caption, Don't Be
    Depressed about Getting OLD! Just Think of the
    Advantages of Old Age.
INSIDE: Like Being Able to Whistle While You Brush Your
    Teeth. Happy Birthday!

COVER: The Professor in the Shoe cartoons, an old bird
    dressed in a baggy jacket and a pair of tennis shoes, is sitting
    at a desk reading a letter with the caption, This Is to Notify
    You That Now That You Are over 30 . . . .
INSIDE: Your factory warranty has run out. Happy Birthday.

COVER: An old man wearing a crash helmet is riding in his car
    with his spectacles down on his nose, looking through a pair
    of binoculars. The caption: I Know You Still Like to Chase
    the Girls . . . .
INSIDE: . . . BUT . . . Do You Remember WHY? Happy
    Birthday!

COVER: A fat puppy dog is sitting upright on a park bench.
    The caption: One Nice Thing about Growing Older . . . .
INSIDE: . . . You Don't Have to Learn Any New Tricks!
    Happy Birthday!

These are only a few examples of ageist humor popular in American society. Ageist images, stereotypes, and myths perpetuated and communicated through common aphorisms, literature, the media, and humor have negative effects on older people and on society as a whole.

The Effects of Ageism

Older people believe that they are useless, out to pasture, nonproductive, sexless, and senile. Bombarded by negative stereotypes and myths, they internalize these perceptions and images and suffer the consequences.

Older people do not want to identify themselves as old. They have an intense fear of growing old just as young people do. Many deny their age and, like Jack Benny, remain 39 forever—dressing and wearing their hair in styles that make them look years younger, in the hope of staying young. These elders are trying to pass, just like members of minority groups who are discriminated against try passing as members of the dominant culture. The denial of aging is particularly common among women, who are judged primarily by outward signs of youth and beauty. Visible signs of aging pose a major threat to their status. In her study of older women, Sarah Matthews (1979) found that older women were ashamed of their age, denied aging, and refused to take on the discrediting "stigma" of being old. Many refused to admit they were old, in spite of the fact that they were in their 70s and beyond.

Ashamed to Be Old

Older adults, confronted in the mirror by wrinkles, graying hair, sagging skin, and other visible signs of aging, feel the stigma of being in a devalued status and feel embarrassed and shamed by their own aging. As they are forced by society to change their age identity and their self-identity and come to define themselves as old, they experience a sense of self-derogation and lowered self-esteem. For them, the American dream of independence, self-sufficiency, success, money, and material possessions is shattered as the specter of dependence and nonproductivity looms large. Many feel dejected, degraded, devalued, demeaned, humiliated, useless, and worthless.

As they come to see themselves as old, with all of the negative connotations surrounding the status of the old in American culture, many feel abnormal, deviant, or marginal members of the culture. As Pat Moore described the feeling in *Disguised,* they feel like an uninvited, unwelcome guest at the family reunion. To use sociologist Erving Goffman's term (1963), they feel they have a "spoiled identity." As a result, many disengage from participation in civic, social, and other groups and become isolated.

Ageism contributes to a sense of helplessness and powerlessness among older adults. If they accept the negative stereotypes and myths about old people, they may come to see themselves in negative terms. They believe they can no longer effectively live life and influence people and their environment. The negative images serve to keep them in passive roles and to limit their attempts at creative, productive pursuits. As such, ageism creates a self-fulfilling prophecy for many older people. An individual who believes she or he cannot learn will never go back to school or engage in other educational or professional training activities—and as a result will not learn. An older man who believes he no longer has the ability to perform sexually will stop initiating sexual contact with his wife, who then may feel hurt and rejected and turn away from him, confirming his fear that he can no longer perform sexually. Betty Friedan (1963), author of *The Feminine Mystique,* and now in the 60-plus group herself, has discovered there is an age mystique just as there was a feminine mystique in America. It is a permeating image of the old as childlike, dependent, passive, sick, mindless, and senile. Older people tend to accept that definition and feel depressed. Their self-esteem and expectations are diminished, just as those of women were before the women's movement.

Ageism oppresses older people, locks them into narrowly prescribed cultural roles, and keeps them from reaching their full potential. Like racism and sexism, ageism results in prejudice and discrimination. One of the best examples of age discrimination is in the workplace. Too often, older workers are the first to be fired and the last to be hired, and they are passed over for promotions and raises. Prejudice manifests itself in many ugly ways, ranging from disdain, dislike, and subtle avoidance of contact with older people to total lack of respect and even outright hatred.

Scapegoats for Society

Ageism results in the use of older adults as scapegoats for all of the social, political and economic problems of the day. Arguments go something like this: The reason the federal deficit is so large is that we pay too much money out in Medicare and social security payments to those aged 65 and older. The reason the health care industry is in such a mess is that sick old people are draining all the health care resources.

By categorizing the old negatively, younger members of society can see the old as different, deviant, not quite as good as the young, and possibly even as less than human. Ageism makes it easier for society to ignore the old and to shirk its economic and social responsibility to older citizens. Ageism blinds us to the many problems older men and women face and keeps older people from receiving the social, economic, and spiritual services they need and deserve. It facilitates control of younger people in power over older people by rationalizing their subordination, exploitation, and devalued status. By labeling the old as different or abnormal, it is easier for other members of the society to deny older citizens access to societal resources and thus retain for the young power, status, wealth, and authority.

Ageism: We're All Losers

Ageism not only has many negative consequences for elders; it has negative effects on younger people and on the society. Younger adults develop a deep fear of and anxiety about growing old themselves. They avoid contact with older relatives, neighbors, and co-workers. As a result, they fail to benefit from the accumulated knowledge, wisdom, and skills that are developed over a lifetime. Contact with another experienced generation is forfeited, a sense of history and cultural continuity is sacrificed, and the generation gap widens.

For society, the failure to acknowledge and utilize the knowledge, wisdom, talents, and skills of older members is a terrible cultural waste. Old people represent one of our greatest untapped natural resources. They hold the keys to the past and to the future. The mistakes they have made are valuable if we are not to repeat these mistakes. Their skills and talents represent a major reserve for business, church, and community leaders. The only adult age group with plenty of free time, the old represent our most important source of volunteers to work in church, social, health care, and other organizations. Old age is a status we will all occupy one day if we live long enough. If left unchecked, ageism will eventually affect all of us.

In *The Coming of Age* Simone de Beauvoir (1972) made an important observation about ageism: "The meaning or lack of meaning that old age takes on in any given society puts that whole society to the test."

3

The Season of Losses

Most people remain active and happy into the last decades of life. Rather than experiencing the final years of life as physically and mentally debilitating, they remain functioning members of their families, their churches, and their communities, fully embracing life and facing each new challenge with courage. The myths and stereotypes about aging and old people do not apply to the majority of elders, who find that their last years contain many wonderful surprises and can be the best years of life. But not everyone fares so well. For these at-risk elders, the passing of time brings physical loss and pain, loss of loved ones and emotional suffering, and other difficult social, personal, and financial losses. These individuals may choose suicide to escape the pain of loss. The following quotation from a 75-year-old man living in a nursing home poignantly expresses how many older people, who have experienced many significant losses in late life, feel:

> I'm no good to anybody. I can't drive. They took all of my money for this place. I can't even go fishing with my boy, and fishing was the only thing I really loved after Martha died. I wish I could just sneak out of this place one time and get my pole and tackle and get in the boat and fish all day long. But, I can't even drive and they sold my boat, too. I took the operation on my legs a few years ago cause they gave me a 90 percent chance of dying. Well, that's why I took the blame thing. And wouldn't you know it's my luck. I didn't die and here I am. I'm no use to anybody. I can't do nothing now but just sit and stare out the window. I'd be a whole lot better off if I was to die. [He did attempt suicide.] (Osgood et al., 1990, p. 53)

Old age has been called the season of losses. The elderly suffer more losses in more rapid succession than people in any other life stage. Many suffer physical and sensory losses: declining health, painful chronic debilitating illnesses, and loss of eyesight and hearing. Others suffer major social losses as they relinquish important roles in family, work, and community. Financial losses are common. Others suffer deep personal losses as spouse, friends, relatives, and pets die. As they age, many people are faced with the loss of freedom and independence, personal autonomy, and personal dignity. They may, through illness, death of a spouse, or financial problems, find themselves dependent on others to meet their needs and may lose control over their own lives.

These losses are a major source of stress in later life. Older adults have less resistance to stress and are more vulnerable to its negative consequences: physical illness, psychological distress and anguish, and even premature death. Older people who lack the personal and social resources to help combat the stresses of aging are at increased risk of depression and suicide.

This chapter explores some of the main losses people face as they age, focusing on the stresses caused by these losses and discussing some of the signs and symptoms of stress in older adults. The major kinds of losses older people experience can be broadly classified into six categories: physical, sensory / perceptual, cognitive, social, financial, and emotional and personal.

Physical Loss

The most frequently condoned suicide among the elderly is suicide because of physical pain and suffering, chronic, debilitating illness, or terminal illness. Individuals in the last stage of life suffer more from physical illnesses then do younger individuals. Seventy-five percent of those aged 65 and older have at least one chronic illness, and more than half of those aged 75 and older have two or more such illnesses. Chronic illness, unlike acute illnesses, are long term and often require medication, changes in dietary habits, or life-style changes. Heart disease, diabetes, osteoporosis, arthritis, and other chronic conditions older adults suffer from often cause pain and suffering. Many older people develop cancer, one of the most dreaded diseases in our culture. Others lose a limb, common in diabetes, lose the ability to walk, lose speech, or lose other physical functions that impair the ability to perform normal tasks of daily living and decrease mobility.

As people age, they experience numerous other physical changes, though some changes are slow and may not be very apparent or restrict their life-style. The hair grays, thins, and may fall out. Teeth may be lost and replaced by dentures. Skin sags and wrinkles. Muscular strength declines. Bones become brittle and break more easily. Joints stiffen. Breathing capacity declines, so climbing stairs, brisk walking, and even yard work and housework become more difficult. All of these changes bring the older adult face to face with the loss of youth and the inevitability of aging.

Physical losses, disfigurement, pain, and suffering place great physical stress on the aging body. They threaten bodily comfort and integrity and may result in a breakdown of personal identity. An individual who has been strong and healthy, full of vim and vigor, and able to function successfully in the environment may undergo an identity crisis when faced with severe physical loss. Pain and illness and diminished physical resources and capabilities may force the older adult to assume a new identity—one of a frail, sick, dependent person who cannot meet the demands of life without help. Pride in one's body and its resiliency may be severely shaken in the face of debilitating disease. Physical loss and illness may cause anxiety and worry, loss of self-confidence and self-esteem, interruption of life activities, and altered relationships with family and friends. The most debilitated—those who cannot bathe or dress themselves or take care of their own toileting without assistance from others—suffer the most. They are humiliated as others dress and bathe them, and they lose their personal dignity under such circumstances.

Sensory/Perceptual Loss

Sensory/perceptual loss in later life is another principal source of stress for elders. All five senses decline: vision, hearing, taste, smell, and touch. Visual acuity is greatly reduced in later life. Night vision is often poorer, and distinguishing certain colors, such as blues and greens, becomes more difficult. Visual loss increases the danger of falls and accidents; makes driving, especially at night, difficult and dangerous; reduces the enjoyment of the beauty of nature, art, and other visual experiences; and hampers effective maneuvering in the physical environment.

Visually impaired elders may find themselves in a dark and frightening place, even in fairly familiar surroundings. Fear of falling and getting lost may lead them to restrict their movement outside the home greatly. Social life may decrease as visual impairment worsens. As vision decreases, even many solitary enjoyable activities—needlework, painting, reading, gardening—may have to be relinquished. As their physical and social life shrinks, visually impaired elders are increasingly isolated.

Hearing deficiencies are common. High-frequency sounds become harder to hear. The intensity of sound must be greater to be accurately perceived by older persons. Hearing loss interferes with normal social interaction with family and friends, who may not talk loudly enough to be heard, and can result in social isolation as the hearing-impaired elder withdraws from social interactions and activities. As hearing progressively declines, many older adults derive less pleasure from television and radio, two favorite pastimes for older people. They cannot enjoy and appreciate music as before, depriving them of a valuable aesthetic experience and source of pleasure.

Announcements over loudspeakers may not be accurately heard. Alarms that signal danger may be unheard and unheeded. Prowlers and purse snatchers may not be heard by hearing-impaired elders. Hearing loss may increase the risk of falls and accidents and make older individuals more vulnerable to attack and crime.

As the senses of taste and smell decline with age, older people have difficulty tasting sugar and salt and smelling food. Food tastes bland, and the pleasure of eating is greatly decreased. Older adults are deprived of the smells of baking bread, fresh flowers, and perfumes and fragrances.

Because tactile senses diminish, older individuals may be less sensitive to hot and cold. Many burn themselves without realizing it, and the danger of hypothermia is greatly increased because older adults may not feel the cold in winter. Older adults may contract diseases such as peritonitis and not realize they are ill because of their decreased sensitivity to pain.

Cognitive Loss

Cognitive loss frequently accompanies the aging process. One of the most common cognitive losses is loss of memory, especially short-term memory. Older individuals who frequently misplace glasses, purses, or keys or forget to turn the oven off begin to question their own competency. Some fear they are suffering from the early signs of Alzheimer's disease. If they forget names or birthdays of close friends and relatives, embarrassment and concern over their loss of mental capacity increase.

Complex problem solving may become more difficult with age. Older people who experience greater difficulty in balancing their checkbooks, completing their tax forms, and organizing their personal and business affairs may become anxious and concerned. Some fear they are becoming incompetent and may lose their ability to manage their money and control their affairs. When a son or daughter assumes power of attorney, many older individuals feel powerless and useless.

If cognitive losses become progressively worse, older adults may feel more stupid and incompetent. Those who feel helpless to control their environment and to manage their own affairs may suffer from feelings of lowered self-esteem and self-concept. Many experience a change in identity if they come to view themselves as incompetent, dependent, and powerless rather than as capable, functioning adults in control of their lives and their environment.

Social Loss

Émile Durkheim (1897–1951), the French sociologist who authored one of the first major books on suicide, argued that suicide cannot be explained by biological or psychological factors alone. Durkheim contended that the major factor in suicide is social. The nature and extent of an individual's social involvement in society is an important determining influence on that person's vulnerability to suicide. According to Durkheim's classical theory, an individual who experiences losses in the social realms of work, family, and community is more vulnerable to suicide than one who has not. Loss of social relationships and social positions and decreased social interaction and social participation place older adults at greater risk of suicide.

Widowhood: A Major Turning Point

Death of a spouse represents a major social loss in late life. Durkheim found that higher rates of suicide among widows and widowers are due to what he called domestic anomie, or a deregulation of behavior assoicated with the loss of a spouse. In other words, when a spouse dies, the widowed partner is left alone with no other person to help structure relationships and to set the boundaries of acceptable and unacceptable behavior. Older people, who may have been married for fifty years or more, suddenly find themselves adrift, searching for a new pattern of behavior and a new style of living without a partner and without a familiar set of guidelines to structure interactions. Such a situation may increase the risk of what Durkheim termed anomic suicide, or suicide that results from the loss of societal control or regulations, leaving the individual to structure the world and find meaning and existence.

Widowed persons are also at greater risk for committing egoistic suicide, Durkheim's term for suicide that occurs when a person is not socially integrated or tied into a major social group such as the family—in other words, profoundly lonely. Lack of social interaction, social support, and social relationships increases the risk of social isolation and egoistic suicide. Loss of a spouse means the loss of a companion, friend, lover, confidant, and partner. Many widowed persons find they have lost their best friend and traveling companion. Eating meals, going out for entertainment, traveling, and other social activities formerly enjoyed with a spouse lose their appeal, satisfaction, and joy when they cannot be shared with a significant partner.

Widowed persons often experience a change in their friendships if couples avoid them now that they are single. Social activities that require a partner—dancing, tennis doubles, card playing—often are no longer available as social pursuits. Widows commonly complain of feeling like a "fifth wheel" in couple-oriented social activities. These social losses compound the isolation of widowed individuals, who are already suffering from the personal loss of a lifelong partner. Widowed males suffer most because there are fewer widowed males to talk to and enjoy activities with. Males, moreover, have not traditionally been the initiators of social activity and, as widowers, are much less likely to go to church or community events or participate in other social groups and activities.

The loss of a spouse also represents a loss of personal identity. A woman who has always seen herself as someone's wife and partner must learn to see herself as a single person. The social roles of wife, cook, and housekeeper, which may have structured her daily existence for many years, must be supplanted by new roles as she carves out a new identity that does not include her former spouse and the life they shared as a couple.

Retirement: A Time of Loss

The loss of the work role in retirement represents another major social loss, particularly for older males. Loss of the work role is accompanied by a loss of companions and structured social interactions and relationships in the work environment. Professional colleagues also may have been golf buddies, tennis partners, and lunch companions outside the office. Retirement may interrupt or alter these relationships. Many males engage in very few social interactions and social activities outside their work.

Retirement brings with it loss of money, status, prestige, and power accompanying the work role. Those who lose the important social role of worker are forced to confront their decreasing opportunity to achieve life goals not already reached. These realizations may produce feelings of despair, demoralization, uselessness, and powerlessness. A man who is primarily integrated into society through his occupational role suffers the most in retirement and is at greatest risk for suicide.

Retirement may result in an identity crisis for some older people, especially those who were totally bound up in their work and had few nonwork interests, activities, or values. For these people, leisure roles and noncareer pursuits are not adequate substitutes for work and are not fulfilling and satisfying. Today's older adults were reared with the work ethic that emphsized the positive value of work and denigrated leisure and idleness. Worth was measured in terms of productivity, and to be nonproductive was a negative position. For these individuals, retirement represents a loss of dignity, self-respect, and status and signifies they are old, useless, and no longer vital, contributing members of their community and society at large.

In his book *Stigma,* Erving Goffman (1963) describes the stigma of occupying a devalued status as a "spoiled identity." In a society such as ours, which worships youth and beauty and highly values materialism and progress, the old have spoiled identities if they are devalued and become victims of negative stereotyping and cultural ageism.

Alvin Toffler in *Future Shock* (1970) characterizes American society as a "throwaway" culture in which the aged are one of our "disposable items." Like paper cups and disposable diapers, old people are viewed as replaceable when they outlive their usefulness. Estranged from their culture and from meaningful roles in family, work, and community, older adults become marginal people—outsiders living on the fringes of their society and looking in from the outside.

Financial Loss

Many older retirees and widowed persons experience financial loss. Loss of money from earned income results in the loss of buying power and, symbolically, loss of personal value, status, power, prestige, and independence.

A lower income means a diminished standard of living and decreased participation in travel, sports events, cultural activities, and other more expensive leisure pursuits. If financial resources fall precipitously, which may occur when catastrophic illness or natural disaster strikes or one lives into extreme old age in an inflationary society, then providing food, shelter, and other daily necessities may become difficult or impossible. The population of homeless elders grows every year.

The loss of money from earned income is only one of the types of financial loss; it can also encompass loss of farm, land, home, car, and personal possessions. Many older individuals are forced to sell property to pay bills or to be able to quality for Medicaid payment for expensive stays in long-term-care institutions. When older people move into smaller apartments or into the home of a child, they may be forced to sell their farm or home, as well as their car and personal possessions. These losses strip older people of dignity, pride, and status. Loss of a home and personal possessions, which are often seen as extensions of self, threatens personal identity and increases the loss of continuity with one's life history.

The older person, now in a dependent position, has lost independence, control, freedom, and privacy. Stripped of these important vestiges of adulthood and anchors of personal identity, older adults are susceptible to feelings of uselessness, powerlessness, dependence, and depression. The risk of suicide is high for such elders.

Personal and Emotional Loss

Personal and emotional losses cause stress for elders and increase the risk of depression and suicide. The loss of a spouse or a child is particularly difficult. Additionally, older people lose close friends through death or geographic mobility and, they experience the loss of beloved pets, which causes more grief than many people realize. Faced with deep personal losses, some older people feel abandoned and rejected, isolated and alone, hurt by the loss of love and companionship. Bereavement can produce such anguish and despair that suicide may appear as a welcome escape from the psychic pain.

The loss of a home or farm and personal possessions are also extremely painful for older persons. Moving from the neighborhood where children were born and reared and where a life was shared with spouse, friends, and neighbors is very difficult for older people. A move into a nursing home or other long-term-care institution is particularly traumatic and, for many, signals the beginning of the end.

As individuals are stripped of cherished pets and personal possessions when they enter an institution, they often lose personal identity, and their sense of self-esteem erodes. Such individuals, who become identified primarily as a patient or resident, lose their individuality and uniqueness. Once institutionalized, they must share formerly private places, such as bathrooms, bedrooms, and dining rooms, with persons they had never met before their move to the facility. Sleeping is often communal, with one or more roommates, also strangers. In the dining room, seats of choice are rare since residents are usually assigned by the nursing or dietary staff to eat with people they barely know and with whom they have little in common. Institutionalization results in loss of freedom, personal autonomy, independence, power and control, and privacy. Removed from the people and places they love and cut off from former social relations and group involvements, institutionalized elders too often suffer from loneliness and social isolation. Powerless to control their environment and to make their own choices, they are particularly susceptible to feelings of helplessness and lowered self-esteem and are at increased risk of depression and suicide.

As the physical, cognitive, social, financial, and personal losses accumulate over the years, many older adults cross what Marv Miller

(1979) terms the line of unbearability: "the personal equation which determines for each of use the point where the quality of life would be so pathetically poor we would no longer wish to live" (p. 8). Older adults who cross that personal, imaginary line either cry out for help or kill themselves.

Jack: A Case Illustration

Jack, a 75-year-old retired white male living in a medium-sized city in New Mexico, has experienced many of the losses just discussed: the loss of his wife of thirty years after a ten-year battle with cancer and a painful death; the loss of his french poodle and faithful companion of ten years, who suddenly dropped dead of a heart attack; the loss of his health, as his own cancer and emphysema have worsened; the loss of his family home and familiar neighborhood and loss of contact with lifetime friends and neighbors when he remarried and moved across the country to live with his new wife; and the loss of freedom, autonomy, independence, personal control, and mobility when he lost 100 pounds and was forced to use oxygen around the clock to breathe. Formerly a strikingly handsome, strong, virile, tall man with a good job and a loving wife and family, in the last ten years Jack has become a frail, sickly scarecrow of a man, fighting for every breath, confined to his home and the oxygen tank he is now wed to for survival.

Born in rural South Dakota, Jack was an only child. He grew up in a closely knit family and attended school in a small community. With his thick, black curly hair and good looks, he was admired by all the young girls around. After graduating from high school, Jack married at age 19 and enrolled in the army in World War II. He fought in the front lines at Normandy on D-Day. While he was serving in the armed forces in Ireland, his mother died. He took a military leave and returned home for a time to mourn. He was close to his mother; her death was a great loss.

After his tour of duty, Jack, now father of a baby girl, returned home, only to find that his young wife no longer wanted to be married to him. They divorced, and he had very little contact with his wife and young daughter after that. A few years later Jack met the new woman of his dreams, a beautiful young widow, ten years his junior, with a 6-year-old daughter. After courting, they were married and spent the next thirty years building a life together. They had another daughter a few years after they married.

Jack went to school to learn to sell life insurance. He scored the highest on the insurance examination, doing better than his young, college-educated colleagues. In addition to high intelligence, Jack's phenomenal memory that enabled him never to forget a face was a real asset in his insurance business. His wife worked as a secretary in an insurance office.

After several moves during the early years of their marriage, Jack and his wife settled in a small town, where they worked and raised their family. Jack traveled extensively for business and with his family for pleasure.

As a traveling salesman, Jack was totally independent and autonomous. He was fiercely independent as a family man and as an individual, making all important decisions about moves, finances, and business affairs. He owned his home and several cars, his passion, and was a good provider.

Active in his church and community, Jack attended church and prayer groups regularly, was an active member of the Veterans of Foreign Wars and the Masons, and even ran, though unsuccessfully, for local political office. He was well known in his community for planting trees all over town. Jack used to say, "Trees live a long time, and I want something to be left in this town after I'm long gone."

When he was in his early 60s, Jack was diagnosed as having a cancerous tumor and underwent difficult surgery. The surgeon removed a major part of the large intestine and bowel, and the operation left Jack with a colostomy. At about the same time, Jack's wife, now aged 45, was diagnosed with breast cancer and had both breasts removed. Both were very ill over the next ten years. Jack had a serious car accident and almost died. Again, he had to have extensive surgery. He developed asthma and emphysema and found breathing, climbing stairs, and walking briskly difficult. He had lip, skin, and lung cancer during these ten years. He reduced his work schedule to half-time, changed jobs to engage in less demanding work, and finally had to quit working. His wife's cancer invaded the bone marrow, and she suffered excruciating pain the last two years of her life. She died at age 55, just after their thirtieth wedding anniversary.

Jack's loss of his wife and his job coupled with his own serious health problems, made life unbearable. Sad and lonely, he did not eat well or take care of the house, and he withdrew from church and community activities and social relationships. He became increasingly depressed during the two years after his wife died, crying a lot and expressing a desire to die.

There were other losses too. His hair thinned and grayed. His teeth were removed. His skin wrinkled; his hands got dark age spots. To a man who had been handsome, these changes were difficult.

As his health worsened, Jack had to reduce his traveling, and he spent much more time inside because he could not breathe the cold winter air. He was afraid of slipping on the ice and falling. This once-mobile and independent man became confined to his house.

Within two years of his wife's death, Jack remarried. A childhood sweetheart, who was also widowed, invited him to spend the winter in New Mexico, and within a few months they were married. The marriage was a convenience for both of them. Both needed companionship; Jack needed someone to cook and clean, and his new wife needed financial help.

The couple decided to live in New Mexico, which meant Jack had to sell his home and possessions, leave the town in which he had built his adult life, and say goodbye to close friends and neighbors. For the thrill and excitement of the new marriage, that seemed a small price to pay, and for the first few years in his new home, Jack was happy. But over time, he began to miss his home town and his good firends. As he came closer to death, Jack longed to go home again. At age 76 now, he is too weak and sick to travel, and he has resigned himself to the painful fact that he will never again see his hometown or friends.

During the last year, Jack has gone downhill rapidly. His asthma and emphysema are much worse, he has lost 100 pounds, and he is on oxygen 24 hours a day. He has been in and out of the hospital several times and nearly died twice. At one point, Jack was too weak to get out of bed; his wife had to feed him, bathe him, and help him to the bathroom. Jack is keenly aware of his own physical frailty. In a recent conversation, he said he is even afraid to go into a public restroom. "I always go look in the bathroom before I go in to make sure there are no big, burly guys in there to strong-arm me and take my wallet. I feel so vulnerable," he said.

Jack's memory is slipping. He cannot remember dates or where he puts his wallet and keys. He has trouble reading and cannot think through a problem. He has lost all of his life insurance policies and some important business papers. He is very aware of these losses, and in frustration one day said, "I'm just losing it!"

Jack eats very little and does not care to live any longer. He has lost his physical strength and stamina, his mental powers, his job, his second wife, his pet, his mobility, his independence, and his freedom. Now he has lost his will to live.

Later-Life Stress

Stress expert Hans Selye (1956) defines stress as phsycial and emotional strain. A good example of a stressful situation is an extended visit by young grandchildren. The noise, disruption, and change in the everyday schedule from such visits are particularly difficult for older adults. After the grandchildren have left, it may still take quite some time before balance is restored in the household and in the older individual.

A stressor is anything that implies or causes threat or trauma. The most common external stressors for older people are retirement, widowhood, and relocation. Common internal stresses for the elderly are physical illness and changes in bodily function and cognitive ability. According to Selye, stressors disturb the equilibrium and produce what he calls the "general adaptation syndrome." That syndrome causes (1) an alarm reaction—physiologically preparing the body for flight or fight, thereby activating the release of the adrenal cortex or corticosteroids into the bloodstream; (2) resistance, in which the body's defenses are called upon to react to the threat; and (3) exhaustion, which results from prolonged exposure to harmful stimuli to which adaptation could not be maintained.

Loss—whether real, threatened, or imaginary—is a stressor that requires adaptation, flexibility, and resiliency if the older person is to cope successfully. Many older people imagine or fear losses that may not occur. Those who hear political discussions about threatened cuts in social security or Medicare benefits may suffer financial stress just from the threat of loss. This is particularly true for those who are already living a marginal existence financially and fear devastating consequences if benefits are cut. Many older people imagine they are suffering from cancer, in spite of medical evidence to the contrary. Some believe they are suffering from Alzheimer's disease when they experience memory loss and mental confusion.

Multiple losses of aging coming in rapid succession put older people under much stress at a time when they are least resistant and resilient. According to Marv Miller (1979), "Whether an older person is able to resolve a suicidal crisis or succumbs to self-inflicted death is very much a function of the ability to cope with stress" (p. 25).

Recognizing Later-Life Stress

One common method of determining how much stress someone is experiencing is a life events inventory. Such inventories provide useful information about recent life events, environmental stresses, and life crises, all potential sources of stress. The Holmes and Rahe Scale of Recent Events, used to determine stress, is a forty-three-item checklist ranging from the death of a spouse as most stressful (100 points) to Christmas and vacations as least stressful (12 and 13 points, respectively), and all other events somewhere in between (figure 3–1).

To obtain a "stress temperature," the person checks off those events that have occurred in the past two years, as well as those that occurred earlier if they are still thought about to obtain a total score. The total score, or "life crisis unit," can range from 0 to over 300 points. A score under 150 indicates low stress, 150 to 300 indicates moderate stress, and over 300 indicates high stress. The higher the stress is, the higher is the likelihood of major illness.

Stress Takes a Toll on the Body

When an individual experiences stress, the body prepares for flight or fight, and the individual experiences emotional and physiological arousal. The heart begins to pound, respiration increases, perspiration increases as palms become hot and sweaty, and the mouth becomes dry. The hypothalamus, part of the subcortex of the brain, activates the endocrine system and the autonomic nervous system. Two hormones, oxytocin and vasopressin, cause constriction in the blood vessel walls and increased sodium retention and blood pressure. The thyroid gland then secretes thyroxin, which increases the rate of respiration, increases anxiety, elevates blood pressure, accelerates the heart rate, and increases gastrointestinal motility of the stomach, which can produce nausea, diarrhea, and ulcers. Under stress there is increased release of hydrochloric acid in the stomach, which causes ulcers, nausea, and diarrhea. Under stress, less saliva is

Rank Event	Average Points	Number of Points That Apply to You
1. Death of spouse	100	_____
2. Divorce	73	_____
3. Marital separation	65	_____
4. Jail term	63	_____
5. Death of close family member	63	_____
6. Personal injury or illness	53	_____
7. Marriage	50	_____
8. Fired at work	47	_____
9. Marital reconciliation	45	_____
10. Retirement	45	_____
11. Change in health of family member	44	_____
12. Pregnancy	40	_____
13. Sex difficulties	39	_____
14. Gain of new family members	39	_____
15. Business readjustment	39	_____
16. Change in financial state	38	_____
17. Death of close friend	37	_____
18. Change to different line of work	36	_____
19. Change in number of arguments with spouse	35	_____
20. Mortgage over $10,000[a]	31	_____
21. Foreclosure of mortgage or loan	30	_____
22. Change in responsibilities at work	29	_____
23. Son or daughter leaving home	29	_____
24. Trouble with in-laws	29	_____
25. Outstanding personal achievement	28	_____
26. Spouse begins or stops work	26	_____
27. Begin or end school	26	_____
28. Change in living conditions	25	_____
29. Revision of personal habits	24	_____
30. Trouble with boss	23	_____
31. Change in work hours or conditions	20	_____
32. Change in residence	20	_____
33. Change in schools	20	_____
34. Change in recreation	19	_____
35. Change in church activities	19	_____

FIGURE 3–1

Holmes and Rahe Scale of Recent Events

Source: Reprinted, with permission, from the *Journal of Psychosomatic Research* 11:213–18; T. H. Holmes & R. H. Rahe, "The Social Readjustment Rating Scale," copyright © 1967, Pergamon Press, Ltd.
[a]Given inflation, we suggest you increase this to $30,000.00.

Rank	Event	Average Points	Number of Points That Apply to You
36.	Change in social activities	18	_____
37.	Mortgage or loan less than $10,000[a]	17	_____
38.	Change in sleeping habits	17	_____
39.	Change in number of family get-togethers	15	_____
40.	Change in eating habits	15	
41.	Vacation	13	_____
42.	Christmas	12	_____
43.	Minor violations of the law	11	_____
	Total Points of Those Items That Apply to You		_____

FIGURE 3–1 (continued)

secreted in the mouth, resulting in dry or cotton mouth. Individuals under stress experience increases in uric acid, serum cholesterol, glucose, and total blood lipids. Waste products build up in the body. Proteins are broken down, and amino acids are liberated. As a result of these changes, older adults under stress are particularly vulnerable to hyperglycemia, elevated blood sugar levels, and diabetes.

Furthermore, a stressor causes the hypothalamus to activate the sympathetic nervous system. In a moment of danger, the autonomic nervous system sends a message to the adrenal glands to release hormones that increase heart rate, blood pressure, and blood sugar to provide a surge of energy needed to meet the threat, increase the force at which blood is pumped out of the heart, and dilate bronchial tubes. When alerted of danger, the sympathetic nervous system increases heart rate and respiration—hence, the pounding heart and rapid breathing when one comes face to face with a dangerous situation. Activation of the sympathetic nervous system also produces a dilating of pupils and bronchial tubes and a release of glucose from the liver. Parasympathetic nervous function is increased. Eye twitches, facial tics, and tremors are evident in individuals under stress.

Muscles tense during physiological arousal, to be ready for fight or flight. Muscle aches are experienced frequently by individuals under stress, especially in the neck, shoulders, and lower back area. Stress causes contraction of skeletal muscles, which can cause tension headaches, backaches, and extreme fatigue.

The stresses of aging require adaptation and reactions to stress, utilizing great amounts of adaptation energy. Older adults under stress may be extremely tired and have low stamina.

Stress Weighs Heavy on Mind and Feelings

Faced with the multiple stresses of aging, many older adults suffer various psychological effects. Some experience anxiety or agitated depression as they become frustrated and overwhelmed trying to cope with many stresses. Failing to see any meaning in the losses they experience, they feel helpless and hopeless and see no purpose in life. Others withdraw from the frightening environment with its multiple demands and show diminished affective response; regressed behavior, such as acting out or clinging dependency; or psychomotor retardation, such as slowed speech, slowed reaction time, and subordination and submission. Disaster victims who experienced the devastating Worcester, Massachusetts, tornado of June 9, 1953, showed signs of regression to almost an infantile level, characterized by memory loss, inability to concentrate, and apathy (Wallace, 1956). Older adults under intense stress behave in much the same manner as disaster victims. Some older adults who suffer multiple losses experience confusion, memory loss, fragmentation of thoughts, impaired judgment, cognitive disorganization, and other cognitive declines. Some of these symptoms closely resemble changes seen in demented or brain-damaged elders.

Table 3–1 provides an overview of the major physiological and psychological reactions to stress experienced by older adults.

Loss and stress are major factors contributing to depression and alcoholism in older individuals, and depression and alcoholism are the two main precipitating factors in later-life suicide. Some older adults are less susceptible to stress and better prepared to cope with stress than are others. Individuals who were raised by loving parents in stable home environments have an advantage over those who were raised in dysfunctional families in which one or both parents were overly-critical and insensitive or were alcoholic, depressed, or had other psychiatric disorders. Older adults who experienced the loss of a parent early in life or who had traumatic childhood experiences may be ill prepared to cope with the multiple stresses of aging.

TABLE 3–1

Physiological and Psychological Reactions to Stress

Physiological	Psychological
Low stamina	Agitated depression
Extreme fatigue	Anxiety
Eye twitching, facial tics, and tremors	Frustration
Extreme fatigue	Withdrawal
Muscle pain, especially in neck, shoulders, and lower back	Subordination
	Diminished affective response
Increased urination	Regressed behavior
Headaches	Slowed reaction time
Increased perspiration	Psychomotor retardation
Gastric hyperfunction in stomach, producing nausea, diarrhea, ulcerative colitis, peptic ulcers	Memory loss
	Confusion
Dry mouth or cotton mouth	Fragmentation of thoughts
Hypertension	Cognitive disorganization
Increased sodium retention	Impaired judgment
Circulatory insufficiency	Decline in other cognitive skills
Rapid heartbeat	
Increased rate of respiration	
Hyperglycemia	
Elevated blood sugar levels	
Diabetes	

Who Copes Best with Stress?

Older adults who have been able to form loving, trusting relationships throughout adult life and have a support group of family and friends are in a good position to withstand the stresses of aging. Those who have been bitter, resentful, and difficult to get along with may find themselves alone and isolated, lacking friends and families with whom to share the joys and sorrows of aging. They are particularly vulnerable to stress and suicide.

Physical health, adequate financial resources, a good education, and a comfortable living environment are all important buffers that serve to insulate older adults from stress. A good personality, memory, and cognitive abilities also protect older individuals from stress. Older adults who are dissatisfied and disheartened, those who have never been particularly positive about life or about themselves, are in greater danger. For these elders, any loss or even threat of loss may be interpreted as life threatening or life shattering. Loss may damage their fragile sense of self-worth and push them further into despair.

Older people who are flexible and adapt well to change are better prepared to face the multiple problems and stresses of aging than those who are rigid and inflexible. Stress requires adaptation; resiliency is an important characteristic of good copers. Those who have learned to replace losses with substitutes that provide meaning are better able to weather the stresses and losses of aging.

4

The Agony of Despair

What I had begun to discover is that, mysteriously and in ways that are totally remote from normal experience, the gray drizzle of horror induced by depression takes on the quality of physical pain. . . . Despair, owing to some evil trick played upon the sick brain by the inhabiting psyche, comes to resemble the diabolical discomfort of being imprisoned in a fiercely overheated room. And because no breeze stirs this caldron, because there is no escape from this smothering confinement, it is entirely natural that the victim begins to think ceaselessly of oblivion.

—William Styron, *Darkness Visible: A Memoir of Madness*

William Styron, at the age of 60, suffered from unipolar depression and almost took his own life. This well-known twentieth-century author grew up near Southampton County, Virginia, where Nat Turner's revolt took place. The story of Nat Turner was the subject of his novel, *The Confessions of Nat Turner,* which received a Pulitzer Prize for 1967. Styron served almost three years in the U.S. Marine Corps during World War II. After the war he completed his studies at Duke University.

His brilliant literary career began with the publication in 1951 of *Lie Down in Darkness,* which won him the Prix de Rome of the American Academy of Arts and Letters. Among his other works are *Sophie's Choice, The Long March, Set This House on Fire,* and a play, *In the Clap Shack.*

Styron had a stable marriage and family life. His wife, Rose, was devoted to him. They owned a beautiful farmhouse in Connecticut and spent part of each summer on Martha's Vineyard.

When he was 60 years old, Styron began suffering from depression, vividly described in *Darkness Visible.* The depression started in

June when he stopped drinking alcohol, a substance he had been abusing for the previous forty years. As often happens after years of abusing alcohol, the tolerance for alcohol greatly decreases in later life, and just a small amount may produce nausea or wooziness. Styron found he could no longer drink without becoming profoundly ill and was forced to abstain from all alcohol. He soon realized that alcohol had acted as a shield against anxiety:

> Suddenly vanished, the great ally which for so long had kept my demons at bay was no longer there to prevent those demons from beginning to swarm through the subconscious, and I was emotionally naked, vulnerable as I had never been before. Doubtless depression had hovered near me for years, waiting to swoop down. Now I was in the first stage—premonitory, like a flicker of sheer lightning barely perceived —of depression's black tempest. (Styron, 1990, p. 43)

In the early stages of depression, Styron began to experience a vaguely troubling malaise. He noticed that the shadows of nightfall seemed more somber and the mornings less buoyant. Activities that had always provided pleasure lost their thrill. Walks in the woods, a favorite pastime, became less zestful. In the late afternoon he was often overcome with feelings of anxiety and panic.

As his depression progressed, Styron experienced other unpleasant sensations. He felt as if his body had become fragile, and he became hypersensitive to aches and pains; nothing felt quite right. These physical symptoms increased his feelings of anxiety, agitation, and unfocused dread.

In the fall, his depression deepened, and the periods of anxiety grew longer and more intense. Styron felt an immense and aching solitude, even when he was with his wife and surrounded by close friends. His voice became faint and wheezy, like that of a very old man. His mental processes, speech, and movements slowed, and he felt like a walking zombie. Even the simplest tasks were an effort. He lost his sex drive. Food lost all its savor. Most distressing were the disruptions in his sleep patterns, along with a complete absence of dreams. He was able to sleep only two or three hours a night and was exhausted every day. At three or four in the morning, he was wide awake staring into the darkness and awaiting the dawn. He could not rid his mind of the line of Baudelaire: "I have felt the wind of the wing of madness."

By winter, he thought about death daily. One early morning in one of his insomniac trances, Styron realized that the condition would cost him his life. He sought psychiatric help, but the depression continued to worsen. He lost all hope, could not sleep, and could not concentrate to write. He felt increasingly anxious, and life had lost all joy and meaning.

In December the thought of suicide gripped him intensely. For years Styron had kept a personal notebook whose contents were private. He had always planned to destroy the notebook before his death or placement in a nursing home. He realized that if he decided to get rid of the notebook, he would have also decided to put an end to himself. One evening early in the month, the moment came when Styron decided he could no longer live with the anguish and despair; he could not get through the next day. He wrote of his depression, "The pain is unrelenting, and what makes the condition intolerable is the foreknowledge that no remedy will come—not in a day, an hour, a month, or a minute. If there is mild relief, one knows that it is only temporary; more pain will follow. It is hopelessness even more than pain that crushes the soul" (p. 62). That evening, when he decided to kill himself, Styron experienced what he called "despair beyond despair," an anguish he did not think possible. He left the room where his wife and friends were chatting to get his notebook. He carefully wrapped the notebook in paper towels, put in a cereal box, and then stuffed it deep inside the garbage can outside. Over the next few days, he made the preparations to die. He saw his lawyer to get his affairs in order. He attempted, to compose a suicide note, the hardest thing he ever had to write, but could not.

Finally, one cold night in December, he slipped out of bed and sat alone in the living room, preparing to end his life. He forced himself to watch a movie, set in late-nineteenth-century Boston, and heard a passage from Brahm's "Alto Rhapsody." The music "pierced his heart like a dagger," and he realized he could never abandon life. He woke his wife up and called the hospital. He was admitted the next day and began the long journey to recovery.

Styron is a good example of an older adult who is suffering from depression and despair. Kierkegaard referred to despair as a "sickness unto death." Depression is the most common mental disorder of later life. Symptoms of depression occur in about 30 percent to 60 percent of individuals over the age of 60. About 15 percent of those aged 60 and older are clinically depressed or have a major affective disorder. Depression frequently causes severe emotional pain that can decrease physical and social activity, reduce functional ability, and precipitate suicide. Depression, the major factor in later-life suicide, underlies about two-thirds of all suicides in older adults. It is often unrecognized and untreated in older people.

Many people equate depression with sadness or the "blues" or think depression and grief are the same. Although they share elements in common, they are not the same condition.

There are basically three types of depression. *Primary depression* results from biological and chemical changes in the brain and the central nervous system or from changes in the endocrine system. It is organically based and has a physical cause. *Reactive depression* is situational; it results from an emotional response to losses, stresses, and changes accompanying the aging process. The third type of depression is *secondary depression*. It occurs when depression is not the major illness but is secondary to other illnesses, such as Parkinson's disease, or to use of medications such as antihypertensives or anti-inflammatory agents.

Factors in Later-Life Depression

Two major types of factors contribute to later-life depression: biological or physical factors and psychosocial factors.

Depression is related to numerous age-associated changes. As humans age, the level and/or activity of many brain chemicals, called neurotransmitters, including acetylcholine, dopamine, norepinephrine, and serotonin, decrease. Decreased levels of the central nervous system biogenic amines, norepinephrine and serotonin, in particular, have been implicated in depression. Changes in the endocrine system, especially in thyroid, pituitary, and hypothalamic function, produce changes in hormone levels that contribute to later-life depression.

Common physical illnesses that cause depression are Parkinson's disease, arthritis, thyroid disease, some viral infections, brain tumors, cancer of the pancreas, strokes, and hypertension. Many drugs commonly taken by older adults can induce depression (for example, antihypertensives, corticosteroids, anti-Parkinsonian agents, anticancer drugs, antiarrhythmics, anti-inflammatory agents, female hormones, antianxiety agents, and analgesics). Malnutrition may also lead to depression in older adults.

Psychosocial factors also contribute to elder depression. Most older depressed individals suffer from reactive depression, caused by psychosocial factors. The many losses older people suffer can cause personal and emotional stress, as well as loneliness and severe depression. Loss and stress often contribute to feelings of helplessness and hopelessness, two major psychological factors in later-life depression.

The losses of people, goals, health, and social roles lead to sadness and mental pain. Older adults who fail to find new sources of satisfaction to replace those that have been lost, may be dominated by feelings of anxiety, despair, helplessness, and hopelessness. Those who cannot cope with their losses begin to lose confidence in their ability to function and to control their own environment. They feel increasingly inadequate and incompetent, they become demoralized, and their self-esteem and self-concept suffer as they begin to see themselves as incapable, helpless, worthless, and useless. Their situation seems hopeless and intolerable. Maurice L. Farber (1968) sees elder suicide as a desperate response to hopeless, intolerable life situations: "Suicide occurs when there appears to be no available path that will lead to a tolerable existence. . . . It is when the life interest is one of despairing hopelessness that suicide occurs" (p. 17). Farber defines hope as the relationship between a sense of personal competence and life-threatening events. Those who have analyzed suicide notes of individuals of various ages have found that the elderly express a sense of hopelessness and what might be called psychological exhaustion. Notably absent is the sense of rage and anger that younger people often express in their suicide notes.

The Picture of Later-Life Depression

Depression in later-life manifests itself with various signs and symptoms. The five major types of symptoms are physical, emotional, cognitive, behavioral, and volitional.

In older adults physical signs and symptoms are the most pronounced. Depressed elders are often tired when there is no physical reason for fatigue. Many depressed older adults experience loss of appetite, eat less, and lose weight. They may experience insomnia or have difficulty getting to sleep, wake up frequently and cannot get back to sleep, or experience early morning wakings. Sex holds no interest for them. Complaints of headaches, muscle aches, backaches, stomach and bowel problems, and racing heart are frequent. The somatic complaints are often clues to depression in older adults. Such symptoms are referred to by physicians as "vegetative" symptoms.

Emotional symptoms of depression or mood changes include sadness or the "blues" and feeling "down in the dumps" or low in spirit. Depressed elders experience unhappiness, emptiness, and dejection. Doctors refer to these feelings as low affect. The depressed older adult usually feels no joy from life and no pleasure in daily activities. Severely depressed older adults feel as if they are in a deep, black pit from which there is no exit. Others feel as if they are enclosed in a room with the walls closing in and no way out except through a passage marked SUICIDE. Depressed elders worry incessantly about financial, health, and family problems.

Cognitive symptoms of depression or depressed thinking take the form of negative pessimistic thoughts about self or about present or future events. Depressed elders feel helpless, hopeless, worthless, and useless. Often they feel guilty, self-blaming, and "bad." They consider themselves to be losers and failures and can see only the negative aspects of events and self. The present and the future look gloomy, bleak, and hopeless. An omnipresent black cloud seems to loom overhead. Other cognitive symptoms of depression are delusions and hallucinations, poor memory, inability to concentrate, difficulty making decisions, and slowed thinking.

Behavioral symptoms of depression are sometimes the easiest to recognize. Speech, physical movements, or gait slows. Hand wringing, pacing, and stooped posture are behavioral signs, as are withdrawal from daily activities and pastimes, lack of attention to dress and grooming, and withdrawal from family and friends. Some depressed older adults become restless and agitated, engaging in hostile behavior such as yelling, screaming, or throwing things. "Geriatric delinquency" is the term used to describe such acting out. Any major change in behavior is a clue to later-life depression. When an older adult who loved gardening no longer wants to work in the garden, it may be a sign of depression. Similarly, when a faithful older person decides church or synagogue is no longer important and stops attending services, it may signal depression.

The final type of symptoms are volitional. Many depressed older adults give up and no longer have the will to live. One depressed older woman called it "turning your face to the wall." Depressed older adults who have lost their will to live are lethargic and apathetic. They show no interest in sex, family activities, personal activities that have always been a source of pride and pleasure, or their physical surroundings. They experience a paralysis of will that may lead to almost total immobility, even to the point where they no longer even care to get out of bed. Table 4–1 summarizes some of the major signs and symptoms of depression in older adults.

Depression or Dementia?

Depression often masquerades as dementia. Many depressed elders are confused and disoriented and complain of memory loss, factors commonly associated with Alzheimer's disease or dementia. Family members and even physicians often mistake depression for dementia, and the depressed older person is written off as untreatable. In fact depression may be an early presenting sign of dementia, an irreversible organic brain disease. It is characterized by intellectual deterioration, memory impairment, and personality disorganization. Alzheimer's disease is the major cause of dementia in older individuals.

Alzheimer's disease results from brain changes—senile plaques in the cortex, neurofibrillary tangles, which are accumulations of pairs of neuronal filaments spiraled around each other, and degeneration of cells in the hippocampus resulting in the formation of intracellular "nacuoules" filled with fluid and granular materials. Demented elders also experience neurochemical abnormalities, most notably a decrease in the enzyme choline acetyltransferase, a marker for acetycholine, a neurotransmitter involved in memory and learning. Two other neurotransmitters or brain chemicals, somatorstatin and substance P, are also depleted in the brains of Alzheimer's victims.

As Alzheimer's disease progresses, memory loss and cognitive impairment become severe. In the later stages of the disease, victims may not remember where they live or recognize family. They cannot think logically or solve even the simplest problem. Agitation is common, as are wandering and getting lost. Personality and emotional changes occur. Some Alzheimer's patients accuse their loved ones of

TABLE 4–1

Symptoms and Signs of Later-Life Depression

Symptoms	Signs
Emotional: Sad, dejected, decreased life satisfaction; loss of interest, impulse to cry, irritable, fearful, anxious, worried; sense of hopelessness, helplessness, failure, emptiness, loneliness, uselessness; negative feelings toward self	*Appearance:* Stooped, sad, hostile, crying, whining, anxious, irritable, suspicious, uncooperative, socially withdrawn
Cognitive: Low self-esteem, self-criticism, pessimism, suicidal thoughts, ruminations, doubt of values, concentration and memory difficulty; delusions: uselessness, blame, somatic, nihilistic; hallucinations: auditory, visual, kinesthetic	*Examination:* Weight loss, confusion, clouding of consciousness, mood variation, bowel impaction
	Severe cases: Drooling, unkempt appearance; ulcerations of skin or cornea due to picking; decreased blinking
Physical: Loss of appetite and libido, fatigue, initial and terminal insomnia, restlessness, hand wringing, picking at skin, constant motor activity, grasping at others	*Psychomotor retardation:* Slowed speech, movement, gait; minimal gestures
	Severe cases: Muteness, stupor, semicoma; cessation of chewing, swallowing, blinking
Unusual behavior: Suicidal gestures, negativism, refusal to eat or drink, aggressive outbursts, stiffness, falling backward	*Psychomotor agitation:* Pacing, awakenings, constipation, pain, restlessness
	Volitional: Loss of motivation, inability to get going, "paralysis of will"

Source: Adapted from Dan G. Blazer II, *Depression in Late Life* (St. Louis, MO.: C. V. Mosby, 1982), p. 21. In Nancy J. Osgood, *Suicide in the Elderly: A Practitioner's Guide to Diagnosis and Mental Health Intervention* (Rockville, Md.: Aspen, 1985), p. 20. Used with permission of C. V. Mosby, Time Mirror Company.

trying to kill them. In the final stages, they lose verbal abilities—there may be no speech at all—and can no longer walk and perform psychomotor functions.

Some depressed elders exhibit symptoms characteristic of dementia. They are confused and disoriented, suffer from memory loss, may demonstrate psychomotor retardation, and have difficulty solv-

TABLE 4-2

Characteristics Commonly Distinguishing
Pseudodementia from Dementia

Pseudodementia	Dementia
Short duration of symptoms	Long duration of symptoms
Strong sense of distress	Often Unconcerned
Many detailed complaints of cognitive loss	Few, vague complaints of cognitive loss
Recent and remote memory loss are equal	Recent memory loss is worse than remote
Attention, concentration often good	Attention and concentration usually poor
Memory gaps common	Memory gaps unusual
"Don't know" answer common	"Near-miss" answers common
Emphasizes disabilities, failures	Conceals disability, emphasizes accomplishments
Makes little effort to perform	Struggles to perform tasks
Does not try to keep up	Uses notes, calendars to keep up
Performance varied on similar tasks	Consistently poor performance on similar tasks
Pervasive affect change	Affect shallow, labile
Social skills lost early	Social skills retained
Orientation tests: "don't know"	Orientation tests: Mistakes unusual or usual
Behavior incongruent with severity of cognitive problem	Behavior compatible with severity of cognitive problem
Symptoms not often worse at night	Symptoms often worse at night
Prior positive psychiatric history common	Prior positive psychiatric history not common

Source: Adapted from C. E. Wells and G. W. Duncan, *Neurology for Psychiatrists* (Philadelphia: F. A. Davis, 1980), p. 93. In Nancy J. Osgood, *Suicide in the Elderly: A Practitioner's Guide to Diagnosis and Mental Health Intervention* (Rockville, Md.: Aspen, 1985), p. 30. Used with permission.

ing problems and thinking logically. *Pseudodementia* is the term used to describe a dementialike condition without primary organic cause or origin. But such depression is not the real thing, even as it mimics it. Unlike true dementia, pseudodementia abates when the older adult is treated for depression.

True dementia is distinguished by such characteristics as the long duration of symptoms; more recent than remote memory loss; poor concentration and attention; struggles to perform cognitive tasks and attempts to conceal disabilities; shallow emotional reactions; consistently poor performance of tasks; and worsening of symptoms at night. Pseudodementia, on the other hand, is characterized by the short duration of symptoms, equal loss of recent and remote memory, good attention and concentration, emphasis on disabilities, pervasive affect change, and no worsening of symptoms at night. Table 4–2 summarizes common characteristics distinguishing dementia from pseudodementia.

5

The Alcohol-Suicide Connection

Rocky: Alcoholic, Institutionalized, and Suicidal

Rocky is a 66-year-old divorced Caucasian admitted in 1984 to a large, skilled nursing facility in the Midwest.* Before his admission, Rocky received treatment for a fractured hip and multiple injuries resulting from a series of falls and for a pulmonary condition at a nearby Veterans' Administration medical center hospital. An initial assessment showed limited ability to walk, unsteady gait and balance, and a visual deficit caused by cataracts. The cataracts were inoperable due to his health. Shortness of breath, even with limited exertion, created a continuous disability, compounded by a long-standing smoking habit that he was unwilling to relinquish entirely. He alternated between oxygen and medication to relieve his shortness of breath and cigarette smoking to satisfy his habit and to alleviate his anxiety about life. As Rocky put it, "If I quit smoking, I might as well die." Rocky, a veteran of World War II and the Korean conflict and a serviceman for thirty years, spends most of his time in a wheelchair.

Rocky was the fourth of eight siblings and one of two boys. As a child he was expected to help with daily and seasonal farm chores. The older brother left home at age 17 to join the service, causing a hardship for his parents. Rocky's parents withdrew him from school in the seventh grade to help meet the demands of the farm and a growing family. Rocky described his mother, a Baptist, as a very religious woman. He was close to her during his childhood years but described his father as a stern man who felt that the farm was his life. Rocky felt differently. When he was 16, he left home to join the military just as his brother had.

During his army career, Rocky married and divorced three times. Although four children were born of these marriages, he has had no contact with two of these children since infancy, and his relationship with the other children is not strong. One of the children visits occasionally, the other seldom. Rocky has expressed his feelings about his children and their lack of attention: "If my children don't have time for me when I'm well, they sure as hell don't have time for me when I'm sick!"

Retirement from the service, combined with a third divorce, were "traumatic

*Reprinted by permission of Greenwood Publishing Group, Inc., Westport, CT, from *Suicide Among the Elderly in Long-Term Care Facilities*, by Nancy J. Osgood, Barbara A. Brant, and Aaron Lipman. Copyright by Nancy J. Osgood, Barbara A. Brant, and Aaron Lipman, and published in 1991 by Greenwood Publishing Group.

79

events" for Rocky, which he tried to cope with by drinking; he refers to his last twenty years of retirement as "alcoholic years": "I became an alcoholic. I drank all my money away. There wasn't a whole lot for me to live for, really. I surprised myself and did live."

The injuries Rocky sustained prior to his nursing home admission were the result of a drinking episode. His first year in the nursing home was difficult for him and for the staff. He was angered and disappointed because of his placement in a long-term facility so far away from his home and his mother, who is old and ill in a nursing home in his home town. His anger extended to his physical incapacity, an altered life-style, and the curtailment of his drinking. These factors contributed to his depression, which was frequent and so strong that on several occasions Rocky openly discussed committing suicide by hanging himself using a belt or sheets.

During the first year in the nursing home, Rocky had frequent episodes of epigastric distress, with nausea and vomiting. He would refuse to eat for three or four days, claiming swallowing difficulties. Some staff viewed the refusal to eat as an attempt to starve to death.

Rocky sometimes remains in bed for prolonged periods. Severe muscle, joint, and low back pain are relieved every three to four hours with a narcotic/analgesic, prescribed and administered over an extended period. Rocky requests the pain medication frequently because "it just makes me feel better." His dependence on the pain medication has replaced his former dependence on alcohol.

Mr. I.: Alcoholic and Dead

After he became an alcoholic, Mr. I.'s first wife divorced him. Later he remarried and stopped drinking for fifteen years. For no apparent reason—even Mr. I. said he did not understand why—he suddenly began drinking again. His second wife, six years his senior, said that when he was not drinking he was an amiable and hard-working man.

For many years, Mr. I. had been a spray painter in a factory. The color of the paint he used last could be seen when he coughed into a handkerchief. Eventually he developed tuberculosis and was in a sanitorium for a year and a half, although several times he became angry and left without medical approval. The top lobe of his right lung was removed and for the rest of his life he experienced difficulty breathing. He had stomach problems for many years, which had been diagnosed as ulcers; however, he suspected he had cancer of the stomach.

Information about two previous suicide attempts was sketchy, but it appeared he swallowed arsenic about thirty years before his death and was saved by stomach pumping. About three years before his death, he swallowed fifteen Valiums and again had his stomach pumped. Throughout his adult life he often threatened suicide.

Mr. I's mother died in a mental hospital. She had been institutionalized six times. Two of her brothers also had been in mental institutions, and another of Mr. I's uncles had killed himself.

Because of his chronic alcoholism, Mr. I. was seeing a psychiatrist at the time of his suicide. Mr. I previously had been institutionalized for a week after he tried to shoot his wife. When he was drunk, he would often beat her. Once he threatened her by saying: "I could go in there any night and choke you to death and there wouldn't be a thing you could do to stop me." On another occasion, he told her: "If I can't live with you, no one will." She finally grew tired of his abuse, separated from him, and was suing for divorce at the time of his death.

When drunk he was not responsible for his actions. Twice he sold his automobiles to obtain money to buy alcohol; he sold one for twenty-five dollars. Besides smoking more than two packs of cigarettes a day for many years, he had become reliant on Valium. Because of his chronic alcoholism, he was receiving social security disability benefits.

A month before his death he wrote a "To Whom It May Concern" letter and placed it in a tin box where he kept important papers. The letter contained instructions stating he did not want any funeral service, flowers, or obituary. He also said he wanted to be buried in a sports shirt and slacks, not a suit.

On the morning of his suicide, he came to his wife's home. He obviously had been drinking and had brought a half-filled bottle of liquor with him. He asked to see their dog and after petting it went out on the steps in front of the house and lay down. He pulled out a gun and showed it to his wife. She struggled to get it away from him, but he still managed to shoot himself in the head. Because her hand was on the pistol when it fired, she received powder burns. . . The last thing the 60-year-old Mr. I. did before shooting himself was take a drink.*

Karl Menninger, the founder of the Menninger Clinic and author of *Man against Himself*, called alcoholism a form of "chronic suicide." Edwin Shneidman of the Los Angeles Suicide Prevention Center refers to alcoholism "playing dead." Others consider alcoholism a substitute for suicide. Alcoholism plays a major role in later-life suicide. The National Institute of Alcohol Abuse and Alcoholism (NIAAA) estimates that one-third of all suicides are alcohol related. Probably many car accidents and other alcohol-related deaths are also intentional suicides, although reported as accidental deaths.

The Problem of Later-Life Alcoholism

The NIAAA (1986) has identified the elderly as a special population at increased risk of alcoholism. Alcoholism is the most common form of substance abuse among older people. According to the NIAAA, 2 to 10 percent of those over age 60 suffer from alcoholism, or an estimated 540,000 to 3 million people. Since alcoholism is a hidden problem and elderly alcoholics, for the most part, are an invisible segment of the older population, these figures probably greatly underestimate alcoholism among the nation's elderly.

Alcoholism in older adults is hidden for a variety of reasons. Older alcoholics are likely to live alone and to drink alone at home. More-

*Marv Miller, *Suicide after Sixty: The Final Alternative* (New York: Springer, 1979), pp. 51–53.

over, because they are less likely than younger people to be married, to work, or to come in contact with police, their drinking problem is not easily detected. Elderly drinkers and their family members often deny and hide their problem. Family members might even encourage older relatives to drink because they believe it is wrong to deny them one of their last "pleasures" left in life. Often physicians do not recognize the problem or are afraid to confront the older adult. Few admit that alcoholism is a problem for an older patient or relative.

Probably no other group of chemically dependent people in America is as misunderstood, ignored, misdiagnosed, and underserved as the elderly. Their alcoholism is concealed behind their life circumstances, attitudes, and values and family members' and professional caregivers' lack of knowledge, misconceptions, and ambivalent attitudes. They attribute symptoms of chemical dependency to aging or illness or to major life transitions. Aging, illness, and life transitions contribute to chemical dependency in the elderly and cause problems for family members, but the chemical dependency dimension itself tends to be overlooked, even when the other problems are acknowledged and dealt with.

Alcoholism promises to be an even bigger problem for future generations of older adults. Many of the current cohort of older people were raised during the prohibition era when alcohol was not readily available and alcoholism was condemned as moral weakness; they are abstainers or seldom drink. Research studies conducted since the early 1970s show a pattern of increased consumption of alcohol in more recent groups of older adults. Future generations of elders have been reared in a much more liberal climate in which alcohol is viewed in a positive, and sometimes glamorous, light. Future cohorts are much more likely to use and abuse alcohol, especially older women. But even if current estimates of the rate of alcoholism among the elderly do not increase for future cohorts, the actual number of elderly abusers will double in the next fifty years because of the projected size of the older population.

Not All Alcoholics Are Alike

Three types of elderly problem drinkers have been identified. *Survivors,* or early-onset alcoholics, have a history of long-standing, unremitting lifelong drinking. *Intermittents* are individuals who had periodic bouts of alcohol abuse in young adulthood and middle age but have not been recognized as alcoholics. In later life, however, they turn to alcohol to cope with the problems and stresses of aging. *Reactive problem drinkers,* or late-onset alcoholics, are those who never drank heavily as young people but began seriously abusing alcohol for the first time in response to the pressures and stresses of later life. About two-thirds of older alcoholics are early-onset survivors, and one-third are late-onset problem drinkers.

Survivors demonstrate the same personality deficits, psychological problems, and failures in coping mechanisms seen in younger alcoholics. They have had a history of depression, neurosis, dependence, apathy, pessimism, anxiety, and low self-esteem; perceptions of inferiority and alienation; lowered aspirations, motivations, achievements; and self-indulgence, self-centeredness, and a reliance on alcohol as a psychological support.

Reactive problem drinkers are less likely to have a history of serious personality deficits or psychological problems. Their drinking is a response to current situations and problems related to aging: a failing supportive social network; financial problems; loneliness, depression, and a sense of loss that result from widowhood or the death of close friends; and boredom, meaninglessness, and loss of status and prestige that accompany retirement. Concern with memory loss, decreased physical functioning, health problems, and loss of independence and personal control are factors in later-life alcoholism. The physical and mental pain of growing older contribute to late-onset alcoholism.

Alcohol: A Poison to Older Bodies

Alcohol is a toxic substance, and alcoholism, if untreated, is fatal. Alcohol has even more devastating mental and physiological effects on older individuals than on younger people. Age-related changes in absorption, metabolism, and excretion of alcohol increase the vulnerability of older adults to the negative effects of alcohol. As a person ages, lean body mass declines, and adipose-tissue mass increases in relation to total body weight. That change, combined with a smaller volume of body water in older bodies, explains in part why older people experience higher peak alcohol levels in body water and increased pharmacologic effects of alcohol. The decreased ability to metabolize alcohol as one ages also increases the toxic effects of alcohol in later life. For a given dose of alcohol, a 60 year old will have a 20 percent higher blood-alcohol concentration. Quantities of alcohol that may be safely consumed by a young person can have serious physiological consequences when consumed by an older person.

Among the many negative physiological effects of alcohol on older adults, it inhibits absorption of B vitamins and blocks vitamin C absorption. Magnesium and potassium are excreted excessively when alcohol is in the body. Alcohol depresses the appetite. Because many older drinkers eat very seldom and often poorly, they may suffer from malnutrition and anorexia. They are more susceptible to anemia and have decreased ability to fight off infections.

Alcohol is metabolized in the liver, and some of the most serious damage caused by alcohol occurs to that organ. Liver disease, fatty liver, alcoholic hepatitis, alcoholic cirrhosis, and liver failure are more common in elderly alcoholics than in younger people. Alcohol also affects the pancreas and the digestive system and can lead to pancreatitis, irritation of the esophagus, gastritis and ulcers, nausea, diarrhea, and vomiting. Finally, elderly alcoholics are more susceptible to cancer of the tongue, mouth, stomach, esophagus, and liver.

Alcohol has a major deleterious effect on the heart and circulatory system. Alcoholic elders are more likely to develop cardiomyopathy, or enlarged heart, coronary artery disease, high blood pressure, angina, and heart attacks.

Alcohol: The Destroyer of Minds

The brain and central nervous system are affected negatively by alcohol. Alcohol slows brain activity. It impairs mental alertness, judgment, physical coordination, and reaction time—increasing the risk of falls and accidents.

Alcohol produces the following effects on the central nervous system: loss of balance; interference with vision; loss of sensation, causing an inability to feel pain; decreased ability to perform mental or motor tasks; delirium tremens from alcohol withdrawal; memory loss; sleep disorders, particularly insomnia and decreased rapid eye movement sleep; and confusion.

Alcoholism causes two major dementing illnesses: Wernicke-Korsakoff and alcohol dementia. Wernicke's is an acute stage of brain dysfunction characterized by pain, gross confusion, staggering gait, weakness in the arms and legs, and cloudiness of perception. Alcohol dementia is an irreversible brain disease characterized by mild to severe dysfunction of intellectual and problem-solving abilities and rigid thinking and stubbornness.

Alcoholism also affects the personality in predictable ways. Common effects of alcohol on the personality include loss of inhibition, leading to risk taking; self-destructive or impulsive urges; mood changes leading to feelings of anger, jealousy, and depression; denial; and self-imposed isolation and anxiety. Table 5–1 summarizes the negative effects of alcohol on the body, mind, and personality.

TABLE 5–1
Negative Mental and Physiological Effects of Alcohol

Effects of alcohol on the digestive system
 Irritation of the esophagus, causing difficulty with swallowing
 Stomach irritation leading to gastritis and ulcers
 Liver failure, hepatitis, and cirrhosis
 Digestive problems: nausea, diarrhea, and vomiting

Effects of alcohol on the circulatory system
 Enlarged heart (cardiomyopathy)
 Irregular heartbeat
 Coronary artery disease
 High blood pressure
 Angina and increased risk of heart attack

Effects of alcohol on the central nervous system
 Loss of balance and coordination
 Interference with vision (tracking moving objects, color distinction, and recovery from glare)
 Loss of sensation, causing weakness and inability to feel pain
 Delirium tremens from alcohol withdrawal (hallucinations and shaking)
 Memory loss and brain damage
 Sleep disorders (sleep apnea and insomnia)

Effects of alcohol on personality
 Loss of inhibition, leading to risk taking
 Self-destructive or impulsive urges, such as personal neglect and violent behavior
 Mood changes, leading to feelings of anger, jealousy, and depression
 Psychological disorders, such as self-imposed isolation and anxiety
 Denial of a problem or distorting reality

Drugs and Alcohol Do Not Mix

In addition to its toxic effects on various organ systems, alcohol interacts adversely with drugs commonly taken by older people, causing serious problems. Seventy-five percent of persons aged 65 and older take at least one prescribed medication. Of the 100 most frequently prescribed drugs, at least half including central nervous system depressants, analgesics, anticoagulants, cardiovascular drugs, and antidiabetic agents, have an ingredient that adversely interacts with alcohol.

Elderly persons who take these medications should never drink. Additionally, many over-the-counter drugs interact with alcohol.

Because of older adults' slower metabolism, interaction with alcohol may occur days after the most recent consumption of the drug. An older adult may drink the day after completing a regimen of drugs, not realizing the drug remains in the system, and experience an adverse drug-alcohol interaction. The combination of drugs and alcohol may be lethal in older adults. Harmful drug-alcohol interactions are more likely to occur among female drinkers, since older women are heavier consumers of tranquilizers and psychoactive drugs. Table 5–2 shows the health consequences of adverse drug-alcohol interactions for drugs commonly taken by older adults.

Factors in Later-Life Alcoholism

A number of reasons lead people to become alcoholics in later life. Some older adults develop painful physical illnesses, such as arthritis, lung disease, or cancer. Drinking temporarily dulls their physical pain, especially when used in conjunction with narcotics or analgesics. What begins as a way to relieve pain and suffering can gradually escalate until the person is dependent on alcohol, drugs, or both.

The many other losses and stresses older adults face—the loss of vital social roles in the family, the workplace, and the community; financial losses; and deep personal losses—lead to loneliness, isolation, and depression that can be overwhelming. If they are alone and lonely, many elders turn to alcohol for solace. Retirement, bereavement, isolation, and loneliness are major precipitants of later-life drinking, and alienation from friends and relatives or abandonment by loved ones are others.

TABLE 5–2

*Alcohol Interaction with Over-the-Counter
and Prescribed Medications*

Medication	Possible Health Problems from Alcohol Combined with Drug
Narcotic pain medication (Demerol, Darvon, Dilaudid)	Central nervous system depression, breathing problems, death
Analgesic pain medication (aspirin, acetominophen, ibuprofen)	Stomach and intestinal bleeding, bleeding ulcers
Anticoagulants (Coumadin, Panwarfin, protamine sulfate)	Bleeding
Anticonvulsants (Dilantin, Tegretol, Valproic acid)	Inability of the drug to control convulsions
Antidepressants (Tofranil, Pertofrane, Triavil)	Reduction in central nervous system functioning
Antidiabetic agents (insulin, Diabenese, Orinase)	Unpredictable, possibly severe reactions
Antihistamines (cold remedies, allergy remedies)	Extreme drowsiness
Antihypertensive agents (Serpasil, Aldomet, Esidrix)	Lower blood pressure than recommended, dizziness
Antibiotics (Flagyl, Chloromycetin, Seromycin)	Nausea, vomiting, headache, possible convulsions
Diuretics (Diuril, Lasix, Hydromox)	Lowered blood pressure, dizziness
Tranquilizers (Miltown, Valium, Librium)	Decreased alertness and judgment, impairment of voluntary movements, breathing problems, possible death

The older person who turns to alcohol is usually suffering from feelings of low self-esteem, powerlessness, loss of control, inferiority, apathy, pessimism, uselessness, and worthlessness. Older persons who have experienced a variety of uncontrollable or unpredictable events—the loss of a spouse, relocation, or diagnosis of terminal illness—may view themselves as helpless to cope with such events and may believe they are being controlled by their environment. Their increased helplessness leads to depression and anxiety, confusion, lowered self-concept, feelings of worthlessness, and the tendency to give up, and they may resort to alcohol use or abuse. Alcohol may give the illusion of restoring a sense of personal control and reduce some of the distress associated with a sense of helplessness.

Many older alcoholics are in a chronic state of hopelessness. The person who perceives he or she has no control over what happens today or in the future and who feels powerless to improve the environment or circumstances is at risk for becoming an alcoholic.

Alcoholism-Depression-Suicide: The Deadly Triangle

The relationship between depression and suicide, between alcoholism and depression, and between alcoholism and suicide is direct (Figure 5–1). Studies indicate that the risk of completed suicides in alcoholics is 50 to 70 percent greater than in those in the general population. Among male alcoholics, some studies report a rate of suicide that is seventy-five to eighty times higher than the rate for the general population. Only about 0.5 to 1 percent of the general population die by suicide, compared to 5 to 8 percent of alcoholics of all ages. Studies of individuals suffering from a major affective disorder, particularly manic-depressive disorder, report that the rate of suicide among this group is more than 60 percent higher than the suicide rate in the general population. Lifetime risk for suicide in the general population is 1 percent, compared to 15 percent for depressives and 15 percent for alcoholics.

Studies of alcoholics reveal that between 30 and 60 percent suffer from depression, and a significant proportion of alcoholics have depressives in their family. Similarly, studies of depressives show that

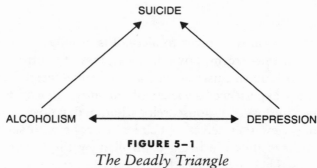

FIGURE 5–1
The Deadly Triangle

compared to the general population, depressives are about five times more likely to suffer from alcoholism, and a significant proportion of depressives have alcoholic relatives. Except for manic-depressives, alcoholics commit suicide more often than any other group.

The second way to establish the links among alcoholism, depression, and suicide is to take a series of suicides and trace how many were alcoholics or depressives. Such studies have been conducted and show that between one-third and one-half of all suicides are alcoholics. In the general population, it is estimated, only about 5 to 10 percent of individuals suffer from alcoholism. Studies of suicides have revealed also that between half and two-thirds of all suicides suffer from depression, unlike the general population, in which only about 15 percent have depression.

Why do so many older alcoholics commit suicide, and why do depression and alcoholism often go hand in hand? To relieve depression and loneliness and to escape from the multiple problems and stresses of growing old, many turn to alcohol. Sandor Rado, a psychoanalyst who practiced in the early 1900s, described a disorder called pharmacothymia, in which drugs are taken by certain people to find relief from intolerable psychic pain. Whether they turn to alcohol or other drugs, these individuals stress the magical qualitites of the drug to bring about a heightened sense of self-esteem and a brighter mood. Although alcohol may help at first to relieve feelings of tension, loneliness, and depression and bolster self-esteem, the euphoric effects are temporary.

Alcohol is a depressant on the central nervous system; ingesting large quantities of alcohol actually increases, rather than relieves, depression and anxiety. It produces feelings of sadness, anxiety, guilt, and remorse. Continuous heavy drinking may result in what Dennis Mayfield and Dan Montgomery (1972) call a "depressive syndrome of chronic intoxication." As older adults continue to drink more and more, their feelings of pessimism, loneliness, worthlessness, and self-pity worsen. Alcohol is a toxin, and its ingestion produces biochemical changes that lead to depression.

Karl Menninger (1938) views both alcoholism and suicide as expressions of a wish to die. Both represent anger and aggression turned inward on the self. Alcoholics and suicides demonstrate a lack of bodily integrity, or lack of concern and care for their own bodies.

The chemical changes that alcohol produces in the brain may alter moods and decrease critical life-evaluating functions of the ego, allowing unconscious self-destructive impulses to gain control. The depressant effects of alcohol may reduce inhibitions and self-control and contribute to the "courage" some feel is a factor in suicide. Dan Blazer (1982), a psychiatrist, points out: "The intake of alcohol frequently blunts inhibitions about suicide and may blunt the potential pain secondary to a suicide attempt." Many older adults who are under the influence of alcohol become impulsive and engage in suicidal behavior, which they would not do if they were not under the influence. Not only does alcohol contribute to impulsiveness, it also produces changes in the brain that result in aggression and aggression against the self is a major factor in suicide behavior.

Continued regular use of alcohol often causes important relationships, primarily among family and friends, to deteriorate, leading to social alienation and isolation. The anger, hostility, and belligerence associated with frequent drinking alienate family members and close friends at a time when the depressed elderly drinker most needs social and emotional support. Coupled with increased isolation and alienation are intense feelings of shame, guilt, pessimism, and lower self-concept, all factors in suicidal behavior.

Signs and Symptoms of Later-Life Alcoholism

Alcohol affects older and younger people in similar ways, so many of the signs and symptoms of alcohol abuse in later life are the same as those of the young. By the time an older drinker is in the late stages of alcoholism, friends and relatives usually are aware that there is a serious problem, but in its earlier stages, alcoholism is not so easy to recognize.

Table 5–3 presents a checklist of major signs and symptoms of later-life alcoholism. Three different kinds of signs point to an alcohol problem: physical, psychological, and behavioral. Common physical symptoms of the problem include hangovers, passing out, blackouts, and loss of control over urination. Hangovers, which occur the morning after drinking, are accompanied by severe headaches, nausea, and sensitivity to noise. In the later stages of alcoholism, hangovers become more frequent and more severe.

Passing out and blackouts are different. Passing out is a period in

TABLE 5–3
Signs of Later-Life Alcoholism

Sneaking drinks

Gulping drinks

Hiding drinking

Drinking more with less visible effects (early stages)

Experiencing gaps in memory

Becoming confused

Unwilling to discuss drinking

Making excuses for drinking

Hiding alcohol to protect supply

Becoming aggressive or abusive, hostile, belligerent

Neglecting appearance and hygiene

Falling repeatedly

Appearing depressed

Neglecting home, bills, or pets

Having frequent car accidents

Eating a poor diet and losing weight

Withdrawing from social activities

Experiencing chronic daytime sleepiness

Demonstrating feelings of low-self esteeem, worthlessness, pessimism, hopelessness

Having intense feelings of guilt and shame

Experiencing changes in sleep patterns, particularly insomnia

Experiencing incontinence

Suffering from the "shakes"

Suffering from hangovers

Having a flushed face, yellowish skin tone, yellow or bloodshot eyes, sallow skin

Having an odor of alcohol on the breath, especially in the morning

Drinking in spite of medical admonitions against it

Experiencing problems with family, friends, or relatives

Experiencing financial or legal problems related to alcohol

Experiencing difficulty conducting normal daily tasks without alcohol which sleep or unconsciousness overcomes the drinker during a party or social event. Blackouts do not result in sleep or unconsciousness. They are periods of alcohol-produced amnesia that may occur after only one or two drinks. During a blackout the drinker walks, talks, drives a car, and functions fairly normally but the next day has no recollection of the period of the blackout. The time is erased from memory, and often a few hours or half a day is totally forgotten. One of the most embarrassing physical signs of alcoholism is loss of control over urination. The drinker who cannot make it to the bathroom in time may be alcoholic. Alcoholics often stay close to a bathroom to avoid such unpleasant accidents. Other physically noticeable signs that the older adult has an alcohol problem are bloodshot eyes, flushed face, yellowish skin color, and alcohol on the breath, especially in the morning.

Psychological symptoms of alcoholism include alcohol dependence, compulsion to drink, and feelings of inadequacy, inferiority, intense loneliness, isolation, and lack of belonging. Alcoholic elders demonstrate a dependence on alcohol. They need a drink to feel good, to relieve tension, or to function. The increased dependence on alcohol contributes to the compulsion to drink. Older alcoholics feel compelled to drink, and they feel they need a drink because they are addicted to the substance.

The behavioral signs of alcoholism are probably the easiest of the three to recognize. The drinking behavior of alcoholics differs markedly from that of other drinkers. Alcoholic elders drink more than everyone else and more quickly. They often insist on having a drink at certain times, such as before dinner or after dinner or on all types of special occasions, such as holidays, sports events, or parties. They insist they need a drink to relieve tension or to cope with problems.

Two other behaviors typical of alcoholics of any age, including older alcoholics, are making promises that are not kept and lying. The alcoholic elder may make many promises about doing better, giving up alcohol, cutting down on the drinking, or abstaining altogether. Lying about drinking often becomes more frequent and more elaborate as the older drinker develops an elaborate system of rationalizations and denial. Denial is the outstanding characteristic of alcoholics. Older alcoholics refuse to see they have an alcohol problem. They refuse to believe or admit they cannot stop drinking even if they wanted to. When the subject of alcohol abuse comes up, the older alcoholic may immediately try to change the subject or become angry.

First the Man Takes a Drink . . .

Alcoholism is a progressive condition in which certain signs and symptoms are more prevalent in earlier stages, and other are more frequent in later stages. The first warning sign for many who may later become alcoholics is increased tolerance or an increased need for more alcohol to produce the desired effect—perhaps three or four glasses of wine to feel relaxed instead of one or two. The increased tolerance usually produces noticeable changes in drinking pattern. Drinking more often or in larger quantities than before or in more different places and at different times of the day may be early signs, as are gulping drinks and experiencing the first blackout. The older person who has a problem will begin to avoid discussions about alcohol and alcoholism.

Most people around the older drinker miss the early signs. Some may notice something but explain away any problem and attribute the noticed changes in drinkers to a "bad day" or to "so many problems to cope with." And older people who drink alone at home may never come in contact with anyone who might recognize a problem.

. . . Then the Drink Takes a Drink . . .

In the middle stage of alcoholism, blackouts are more frequent, hangovers increase in frequency and intensity, consumption of alcohol increases, and more drinking takes place daily at more different times. The older drinker may try to ensure that alcohol is always available and may begin sneaking drinks, hiding the supply, or having a drink in the morning.

At this stage the older drinker experiences a phenomenon that is the major factor that sets alcoholics apart from other drinkers: he or she loses control and can no longer regulate how many drinks he or she will take. The person who determines to have only one drink at the party and ends up drunk has lost control. At that point alcoholics are powerless over alcohol. An old Chinese proverb about the relationship between man and alcohol states it this way:

First the man takes a drink
Then the drink takes a drink;
Finally the drink takes the man.

. . . *Finally the Drink Takes the Man*

As alcoholism progresses, the drinker may drink for days at a time, getting helplessly drunk. Remorse and guilt overtake the drinker who, when sober, realizes the mess he or she has made. The older alcoholic makes more excuses and alibis for the increased drinking. Attempts to stop result in repeated failure, which increases feelings of guilt and remorse. Family and friends become alienated as the alcoholism progresses.

By the late stages of alcoholism, family, friends, and associates are usually aware of the seriousness of the problem. The alcoholic elder is totally dependent on alcohol and cannot function without it. Many remain nearly always drunk, they are often slovenly and dirty, and their house may be a filthy mess. Benders become a permanent part of life. The older alcoholic develops tremors, a nervous condition that produces uncontrollable shaking. Drinking smaller amounts of alcohol results in higher concentrations of alcohol in the bloodstream. The alcoholic elder who could always drink more than others and hold liquor now gets drunk on a relatively small amount of alcohol.

Lying about drinking behavior is a regular occurrence, and a deterioration in the ethical system occurs. Nothing matters anymore except having the alcohol. At that point those friends and family who remain may become even more alienated from the older alcoholic, who also may experience problems with the law and financial problems related to alcohol.

Some common telltale signs of alcoholism during the middle and late stages of alcoholism include frequent injuries to the self, falls and accidents, bruises on the back of the hands or at furniture level, and burns on the hands and chest.

Clues to Later-Life Suicide

Most older people who commit suicide have been suffering for a long time and probably have been sending out signals warning of their impending act. Nevertheless, these suicidal clues and warning signs may go unrecognized.

Suicides share many commonalities, including family history factors, feelings, and emotions. Understanding the commonalities among suicidal people is important for accurate recognition of suicidal individuals. Suicidal elders, like suicidal people of other ages, often give clues to their impending suicide, and these clues tend to be similar in content. Accurately perceiving these clues and interpreting them as warning signals may help save the life of a troubled elder.

Myths about Suicide

MYTH 1: Suicide happens without warning.

A major myth about suicide is that it happens without warning. In fact, most older people who commit suicide give clues and warnings regarding their intentions.

MYTH 2: Talkers are not doers.

Another major myth is that people who threaten or talk about suicide do not carry through. But most older people who talk about killing themselves eventually do. Talk of suicide and suicidal threats are major clues to future suicides in the at-risk older population.

MYTH 3: *Those who try and fail will not try again.*

The myth that those who attempt suicide and survive will not try again is particularly dangerous because most older adults who attempt suicide later attempt again, and usually succeed. Unlike younger adults, older adults are not suicide attempters; they are suicide completers. Most are not crying out for help or manipulating others through a suicide attempt. They are deadly serious about their intention. If their attempt fails and they are rescued, it is usually because they were too physically frail to carry out the act or were discovered. One of the major clues to suicide in the older age group is a previous suicide attempt.

MYTH 4: *The rich and the poor are particularly vulnerable.*

The myth that suicide is more common among the rich or the poor is contradicted by the truth that suicide is democratic. Riches are no protection against suicide, neither is suicide always the curse of the poor.

MYTH 5: *All suicides are insane.*

Although depression and other forms of mental illness often precipitate suicide, not all suicides are mentally ill. Some suicides, particularly those suffering from intense physical pain, do not have mental illness and are in fact acting quite rationally.

MYTH 6: *Suicidal people want to die.*

Most suicidal individuals have mixed feelings about living and dying; they are ambivalent. Suicidal elders may be more intent on dying than younger adults who are suicidal but nevertheless simultaneously want to live and be rescued yet want to die.

MYTH 7: *Alcoholics don't kill themselves.*

The myth that alcoholics rarely commit suicide is contradicted by the statistics: about one-third of all suicides are alcoholics. Clearly alcoholics are at increased risk for suicide.

MYTH 8: Suicide is in the genes.

There is a myth that suicide is inherited. Although a family history of suicide is present for many suicidal people, there is no scientific evidence that suicide is inherited or transferred genetically from parent to child. Suicide of a parent or grandparent may leave a negative legacy for children and grandchildren, who may also view suicide as an appropriate solution to life's problems. Suicide may be a learned behavior, but there is no evidence that the tendency toward suicide is passed down genetically.

MYTH 9: If you get better, the crisis is over.

Improvement after a suicidal crisis does not mean that the risk of suicide is over; nothing could be further from the truth. The majority of suicides occur within three or four months of a suicidal crisis, just when it appears that the person is getting back to normal. During that time of seeming "improvement," the suicidal individual has the psychomotor energy to take action on morbid thoughts and feelings. Suicide is an express danger during such periods.

MYTH 10: Talking about suicide gives someone the idea.

The myth that mentioning suicide may give the person the idea is wrong. Asking directly about suicidal intent, ideas, and feelings may serve to minimize the feelings of anxiety and be a preventive measure. Allowing an older adult to talk about suicide and to express feelings of pain and depression may be just what the older person needs to feel better.

MYTH 11: Once suicidal, always suicidal.

It is not the case that once an individual is suicidal, he or she will always be suicidal. Usually the period of feeling desperate and self-destructive lasts only about six weeks. If the older person can be treated for depression, alcoholism, or both and learn successful ways to cope with the stresses of aging, suicide may no longer be considered as an option.

Common Characteristics of Suicides

Although each suicidal person and each suicidal crisis is unique, there are common features. Individuals who die by their own hand are more likely than others to have a family history of suicide. Social learning theorists suggest that suicide is a learned behavior and is influenced by the environment in which one lives. Suicidal acts of significant others send a message to those left behind that suicide is one possible solution to problems.

Another common factor in the family background of people who commit suicide is something that has been termed the "death trend." Those who commit suicide are much more likely than others to have experienced the death of a loved one in early life, usually before age 12. A significant loss, as the loss of a mother, in childhood may leave deep emotional scars that never heal. In his self-analysis of his own depression and self-destructive feelings, William Styron concluded that the death of his mother when he was a child was probably a major factor.

Individuals who commit suicide are more likely than other people to come from dysfunctional families. Critical, domineering parents are detrimental to children, and these children as adults may still suffer from feelings of inadequacy, low esteem, and worthlessness instilled in them by such parents. Ernest Hemingway's mother was a critical woman who dominated her son and controlled his father, a weak, ineffectual man who also committed suicide.

A family history of alcoholism, depression, or mental illness is characteristic of those who commit suicide. Older adults who take their lives are more likely than those who do not choose suicide to come from families in which parents, grandparents, or siblings suffered from alcoholism, depression, or some other form of mental illness. Children of schizophrenics have an increased risk of suicide.

In addition to sharing certain aspects of family history, suicides have other common characteristics. Edwin Shneidman (1985) has identified ten common characteristics of suicide (table 6–1).

1. *Psychological pain.* The pain of unbearable emotions and anguish is what the suicidal person is seeking to escape. Individuals suffering the indignities and cruelties of German concentration camps most certainly experienced the intense psychological pain confront-

TABLE 6–1

Ten Common Characteristics of Suicide

1. Unbearable psychological pain is the common stimulus.
2. Frustrated psychological needs is the common stressor.
3. The common purpose is to seek a solution.
4. Cessation of consciousness is the common goal.
5. The common emotion is hopelessness-helplessness.
6. Ambivalence is the common internal attitude.
7. The common cognitive state is constriction.
8. Communication of intention is the common interpersonal act.
9. The common action is egression.
10. The common consistency is difficulty with lifelong coping patterns.

ing the suicidal person. Viktor Frankl, a survivor of the camps, has described the intense psychic pain experienced by those separated from home and loved ones, stripped of all personal possessions and human dignity, forced to live like animals in a cage, waiting for death. Whether older people's mental pain is the result of the loss of a loved one, the loss of youth, or the loss of health and strength, they tend to share in common unendurable psychological pain. Suicide represents one way to end their mental pain by stopping the flow of consciousness.

2. *Frustrated needs.* According to Shneidman, the common stressor in suicide is frustrated psychological needs. All individuals need to feel loved, respected, wanted, and needed. They want to be autonomous, competent, and successful and to avoid criticism, humiliation, and shame. When any of these needs is thwarted, the older person can become extremely frustrated, with suicide a possibility.

3. *Suicide as a solution.* Shneidman contends that the common purpose of suicide is to seek a solution; that is, suicide seems to be a way out of a difficulty, crisis, or intolerable situation. The older adult who chooses suicide does not see any other answer. An older person who has lost his or her job through retirement and is having difficulty paying bills on a reduced income may not see any answer to these increasing financial troubles except suicide.

4. *Release from Pain.* The common goal of suicide, according to Shneidman, is cessation of consciousness. An individual suffering - intense anguish often fears the mental pain will worsen and may long for release from painful thoughts, feelings, and emotions, fearing, moreover, that if the mental pain is not stopped, insanity is not far behind. Such a tormented individual sees suicide as the way to stop the flow of consciousness, thereby ending the mental suffering.

5. *Hopelessness and helplessness.* Suicides tend to feel hopeless and helpless. They feel helpless to change the situation, typically thinking, "There is nothing that can be done to help me; nothing that can be done to change things; no one can help ease the pain." Older people who commit suicide see their situation as hopeless; more important, they view the future negatively. Things will never change and will never get better, they fear.

6. *Ambivalence.* The suicidal person is of two minds: both wanting to die yet wanting to have the pain relieved so he or she can live. Many individuals who survive a serious suicide attempt later admit that even as they made the attempt and it was too late to turn back, they were sorry for their action and wished to live. Ambivalence is usually present up to the last moment of the actual suicidal act.

7. *Tunnel vision.* Shneidman identifies the common cognitive state in suicide as constriction of affect and intellect, commonly referred to as tunnel vision because the suicidal person has a narrow perspective. Everything is black or white. The suicidal person sees only two options: live and suffer, or commit suicide and escape suffering and pain. The options between these two extremes are not perceived. In fact, such dichotomous thinking is characteristic of suicidal people. Everything is good or bad, right or wrong. Shneidman gives the following advice: "Never kill yourself when you are suicidal. It takes a mind capable of scanning a range of options greater than two to make a decision as important as taking one's life."

8. *Suicidal communication.* Shneidman notes the common interpersonal act in suicide is of communication of intention. The older person who attempts or completes suicide is sending a message—perhaps a distress signal, a plea for help, or a statement about the intolerability of life.

9. *Escape.* The common action in suicide is egression, or escape. When life becomes too difficult, the suicidal person tries to escape permanently. Suicide is not just an expression of the wish to get away

for a while or the need for respite; it is an expression of the need to end the intolerable physical or psychological pain or the unbearable life situations and problems.

10. *Poor coping patterns.* The final commonality is that suicide is a continuation of lifelong coping patterns. Individuals who commit suicide in later life have a history of coping poorly with the problems and stresses of life at earlier stages. For example, a young adult who cannot face problems at home or at work and turns to alcohol or drugs is ill prepared to cope successfully with the problems and stresses of growing old.

Clues to Suicide

Those who are thinking about suicide usually give clues of their intentions. Research studies of completed suicides bear evidence: more than 75 percent of those who take their own lives gave clues, and often several times to several different people, particularly family members, friends, and doctors. Clues may be verbal or behavioral; sometimes traumatic situations provide clues.

The fact that many older adults give hints before committing suicide means that in many cases suicide is preventable. One statement about suicide or changes in a particular behavior may not be a clue. Rather, it is important to look for clusters of clues in several areas and to view clues in the broader context of life history, recent life events and stresses, and past and current coping capabilities.

Although many suicidal elders give recognizable clues to suicide, their warning signals often go unheeded by family members, friends, and physicians. In his in-depth investigation of more than 300 completed suicides in Arizona, Marv Miller (1978) discovered that more than half of the suicides gave verbal or behavioral clues but many relatives of the suicide did not recognize the clues.

Why are clues to suicide missed? Sometimes a concerned loved one hears clues but cannot believe the troubled elder is serious. Others hear clues or see drastic changes in behavior but are baffled and confused by what they see and hear. Not understanding the seriousness of the situation, they often deny the clues and pretend they do not exist. Still others hear and see clear clues and choose to ignore them, either out of lack of concern, or from perhaps a subliminal or conscious desire for the death of a spouse or parent, or because of lack of time to deal with the problems. Physicians too may fail to respond to clear clues. About 75 percent of older suicides visit a physician within a month, sometimes within a week or day, of taking their own lives.

Clues to suicide fall broadly into four types: syndromatic, verbal, behavioral, and situational. Syndromatic clues refer to those syndromes (constellation of psychological symptoms) most related to suicide, particularly depression and alcoholism. It is important to recognize signs and symptoms of each in order to pick up syndromatic clues. (See table 6–2.)

Mood Changes Signal Dangers

Any major change in mood or behavior may signal depression in older adults. The major symptoms are changes in sleep patterns, particularly insomnia but also early morning waking and frequent waking; changes in eating habits, particularly loss of appetite and weight loss; somatic complaints such as headaches, upset stomach, constipation, backaches, and neck aches; mood changes, particularly sadness, lethargy, and apathy; loss of interest in usual activities; and loss of energy and fatigue.

Alcoholism is the other identifiable syndrome related to suicide. The major signs and symptoms are increased drinking, physical dependence on alcohol, loss of control over drinking, morning drinking, lying and denial, hiding liquor, sneaking drinks, drinking in spite of medical admonitions against it; blackouts, hangovers, and unexplainable cuts, scratches, bruises, and cigarette burns on body and clothes.

Listen for Clues

Suicidal elders typically give verbal clues—statements they make before they commit suicide. Some verbal clues are almost shouted, and others are barely a whisper; some are very blatant, and others are in coded form; some are spoken in a casual, offhanded fashion, and others are uttered seriously. All are important warning signs, and none should be ignored.

Direct verbal clues are just that: "I am going to kill myself," "I want to end it all," "I'm calling it quits—living is useless." Some ver-

TABLE 6–2

Clues to Suicide

Syndromatic clues

  Depression

    Change in sleep patterns

    Loss of appetite and weight loss

    Complaints about illnesses, real or imaginary, or complaints about body aches and minor or main physical problems, real or imaginary

    Mood changes (sadness, lethargy)

    Loss of interest in usual activities

    Loss of energy and fatigue

  Alcoholism

    Increased drinking

    Physical dependence on alcohol

    Loss of control over drinking

    Early morning drinking

    Lying and denial

    Hiding liquor

    Sneaking drinks

    Drinking in spite of medical admonitions against it

    Blackouts

    Hangovers

    Cuts, scratches, bruises, cigarette burns

Verbal clues

    "I am going to kill myself."

    "I am going to commit suicide.

    "I want to end it all."

    "I've had it"

    "I've lived long enough. No more."

    "I'm tired of life."

    "I'm tired of living."

    "My family would be better off without me."

    "Nobody cares about [loves] me."

    "Who cares if I'm dead anyway?"

    "I won't be around much longer."

    "Pretty soon you won't have to worry about me anyway."

Behavioral clues

    Previous suicide attempt

    Buying a gun

    Stockpiling pills

    Giving away money or personal possessions

    Loss of interest in favorite activities, church, or family

    Making or changing a will

TABLE 6–2 (continued)

Making funeral plans
Suspicious behavior

Situational clues
Death of a spouse, child, or close friend
Death of a pet
Major move
Diagnosis of a terminal illness
Retirement
Flare-up with a friend or relative

bal clues are not quite so direct but nevertheless signal the intent to die: "I'm tired of living," "I can't go on anymore," "Who cares if I'm dead anyway?" "My family would be better off without me," "No one cares about/loves me," "I'm no good to anybody. My life's a total waste."

Verbal clues in coded form require interpretation to detect self-destructive interest: "I won't be around much longer," "Pretty soon you won't have to worry about me," "It was good, but we all have to go sometime," "I won't need another appointment, doctor," "If I don't see you again, thanks for everything."

Watch What They Do

Behavioral clues are actions, with the most revealing being a previous suicide attempt. Most older people who attempt suicide and fail try again within two years and usually succeed.

Any major change in behavior may signal suicide. Older adults who have been involved in church activities and stop attending services may be giving a clue. Older adults who have been very close to family and involved in many family activities and outings and suddenly withdraw may be giving signals. Those who always loved gardening, dancing, or some other activity and lose all interest in it may be giving clues.

Common behavior that may signal suicidal intent includes buying a gun, particularly if for the first time; giving away money or valued personal possessions such as jewelry, pets, or antiques; stockpiling pills; making or changing a will, particularly with some urgency; taking out insurance or changing beneficiaries; making funeral plans; or yelling, screaming, and throwing things.

Some behaviors may occur close to the time of the suicide. The older individual who has always kissed the spouse goodbye when leaving the house and fails to do so may be giving a clue, as is the older person who has always faithfully taken a bag lunch when leaving for the day and "forgets" the lunch. Suspicious behavior, such as going out at atypical times of the day or night may provide a clue. The older person who engages in such behavior may be buying a gun or trying to determine where to commit the act.

The Straw That Breaks the Camel's Back

In some cases, the situation of the older person provides a clue to impending suicide—for example, death of a spouse, child, or close friend; death of a beloved pet; a move to a new home or apartment, a nursing home or adult home, or with children or other relatives; retirement; diagnosis of terminal illness; or a major flare-up with a close friend or relative. Many older adults who face these situations manage to adjust; others are devastated and choose to take their life. These situations often are the straw that breaks the camel's back— the event that pushes an individual, who is already on the edge, over the precipice.

Clues in the Case Histories

An examination of some of the cases of suicide in later life already presented in this book reveals many of these clues. In the case of Ernest Hemingway, both major syndromes related to suicide—depression and alcoholism—were present. Hemingway recognized his depression but was unable to climb out of the bottomless pit it represented. Some of the major signs of his depression included loss of appetite, difficulty in sleeping, withdrawal from family and friends, and giving up of favorite activities such as bullfighting and international travel.

Hemingway's alcoholism is well known to students of literature. In his later years, he was often drunk. His physician advised him to stop drinking, but Hemingway persisted. His wife and close friends were worried about his increasing abuse of alcohol and frequent bouts with depression. Hemingway experienced such difficulty in concentrating that he was unable to write or at times even to think coherently, probably as a result of his increased drinking and deep depression. Shortly before committing suicide, Hemingway began to hallucinate and to have paranoid delusions, probably related to his alcoholism.

Hemingway verbally signaled to his wife, Mary, and his good friend, A. E. Hotchner, that he was depressed and in despair, and he signaled his suicidal intentions. Shortly before he committed suicide, Hemingway told Hotchner, "Man is not made for defeat. He can be destroyed, but not defeated."

Hemingway gave behavioral clues. He had flirted with death throughout life, fighting bulls and wrestling lions, flying in small planes over African bush under dangerous conditions, and big game hunting on dangerous safaris, and he had made a previous suicide attempt using a gun. Other behavioral clues became evident nearer the time of his death. He withdrew from family and friends, spending hours alone in his room and even eating there alone. He gave up traveling and other activities he had always loved to spend more and more time at home. He became extremely dependent on his wife toward the end of his life. He no longer could think coherently and creatively and had difficulty completing writing assignments.

Situational clues abounded. In one year Hemingway lost almost every significant other in his life: his grandson, mother, former wife, editor, and best friend. He survived two airplane crashes, which left him with serious injuries and unrelenting pain. His general health also failed. As his eyesight declined, he feared the prospect of going totally blind.

The clues were evident in the case of Dr. Alice Sheldon, who killed her husband and then herself. She had verbalized her intent to kill herself to close friends for the last twenty years of her life and revealed it in letters. Eleven years before the murder-suicide, Alice Sheldon wrote to a friend: "I had always meant to take myself off the scene gracefully about now while I am still me. And now I find I can't, because to do it would mean leaving him alone, and I can't bring myself to put a bullet through that sleeping head—to take him too, when he doesn't want to go." Later she wrote a book expressing such intentions. The couple had made a suicide pact agreeing to die if life became too difficult for one or both of them.

Behaviorally, Alice Sheldon gave up growing orchids, one of the passions of her life, and became a recluse. The situational clues were also present: the loss of her mother and the revelation, against her wishes, of her identity as a writer, her loss of physical health and vigor, and increased pain and suffering due to chronic lung disease and a mitral valve replacement.

In chapter 3 we encountered Jack, a suicidal elder who also gave clues to his intentions. He suffered from depression, particularly after the loss of his wife of thirty years. Jack was sad and cried continually; he expressed feelings of intense loneliness and an inability to go on without his wife. He lost his appetite, and his weight fell by 100 pounds. He withdrew from religious, family, and social activities; gave up traveling, his favorite activity; and stayed at home more and more, spending endless hours alone watching television while lying in bed. Some of these changes doubtless occurred because of Jack's increasingly poor health, but his deep depression probably also contributed to his withdrawal and relinquishment of favorite activities—behavioral clues to suicide.

The verbal clues were there too. Jack spoke openly of wanting to die after his wife died. After remarrying, when he became very ill, he expressed his feelings of physical vulnerability and loss of strength and vitality. Situational clues important in the last decade of Jack's life included the loss of his wife and a beloved pet; retirement and loss of income; a move away from his family home and long-time friends and neighbors to live in another state with his new wife; and declining physical health due to emphysema and lung disease and a diagnosis of cancer.

The major clue with William Styron was his deep depression. He experienced serious disturbance in his sleep patterns and in the later stages of the depression was able to sleep only two or three hours a night; he was exhausted every day. Styron's depression manifested itself in somatic or physical complaints. He had aches and pains and became hypersensitive about them; his voice became faint and wheezy. He moved and spoke more slowly and lost his sex drive. Styron thought of death often and had many suicidal ruminations.

As his depression worsened, Styron gave behavioral clues. He withdrew from his wife and friends, lost interest in activities that previously had provided pleasure, and experienced increasing difficulty in concentrating and writing. The most obvious behavioral clue was his careful disposal of his personal notebook. Destroying such a meaningful part of his life was an important clue that he intended to commit suicide.

7

Keys to Suicide Prevention

As the rate of suicide among older adults continues to rise, suicide prevention becomes increasingly important. The search for prevention keys begins with individuals and continues to society. Some older people are protected from depresssion and suicide; others are particularly vulnerable. What individual traits, characteristics, personal habits, or life-styles help older adults weather the storms of life and age successfully? These protective factors, once identified, may be nurtured in at-risk elders to reduce their risk of suicide. The first part of this chapter focuses on characteristics of people who are survivors; they are adequately prepared to meet the challenges of life and are healthy, successful, zestful, and vibrant into later life.

The responsibility for suicide prevention cannot rest solely upon older adults themselves. Society must help protect them from self-harm through education, outreach, gun control, and similar other measures. Societal measures of suicide prevention are the subject of the second part of this chapter.

Individual Factors

Older adults experiencing what Halpert Dunn (1961) called "high-level wellness" are protected from depression and suicide. High-level wellness encompasses much more than optimum physical health and fitness and the absence of disease. It involves "progresses toward a high potential of human functioning; an open-ended and ever-expanding tomorrow with its challenges to live at a fuller potential; and the integration of the whole being of the individual—body, mind, spirit—in the functioning process" (p. 9). In other words, it is a condition of feeling vibrant, energetic, and possessing a true sense of joy and a zest for living.

High-level wellness is possible only if one is free to realize one's personal uniqueness through creative expression. Dunn viewed the imagination as the greatest asset for achieving high-level wellness. Imagination equips individuals for meeting challenges and solving problems and is the means by which people can explore their future.

The Greek ideal long ago of a healthy mind in a healthy body suggested that physical and mental health are entwined inextricably. More recently the concept of holistic health suggests the intimate interrelationships of body, mind, spirit, and emotion in contributing to health. The idea of holistic health is embodied in the definition of health published in 1974 by the World Health Organization (WHO): health is a "state of complete physical, mental, and social well-being and not merely the absence of disease and infirmity." That definition reflects the concern for the individual as a total person and equates health with productive, creative living.

Holistic health focuses on the wholeness of the person and the need for balance and harmony within the physical, mental, social, spiritual, and emotional aspects of a person's life-style, behavior, and environmental relationships.

Physical fitness and optimum physical functioning are the cornerstones of good health in later life and contribute to sound emotional health, which is essential if the older individual is to cope successfully with the stresses and losses of aging and remain happy, confident, self-assured, and in control. The social component of health involves close, loving relationships and social supports to protect the older person from loneliness, isolation, depression, and suicide. Just as important to high-level wellness in later life is good spiritual health. The spiritual dimension encompasses such intangibles as a sense of purpose and meaning in life, hope, courage, and the will to live.

Physical Health

Three major components of physical health and functioning are diet and nutrition, physical exercise, and stress management.

Eating Right to Stay Healthy and Happy. A well-balanced, nutritious diet is important at any age and particularly so in later life.

Older adults need a variety of foods from each food group daily: two or more servings of dairy products; two or more servings of protein; four or more servings of grains and cereals; and four or more servings of fruit and vegetables.

In later life the body tends to deplete certain vitamins and minerals, paticularly vitamins B and C, iron, potassium, and calcium. Vitamin C is essential to fight off infections and help prevent internal stress from disease. Vitamin B, iron, potassium, and other trace minerals help to mitigate the negative effects of stress and prevent exhaustion, irritability, and lethargy. Citrus fruits, green leafy vegetables, lentils, fish, bananas, potatoes, brewer's yeast, wheat germ, and whole grains provide all of the vitamin C, Vitamin B, and minerals needed to avoid or fight stress.

Certain foods should be avoided. Refined sugars interfere with the absorption of potassium, vitamin C, and B-complex vitamins. Salt drives potassium out of the cells, resulting in exhaustion and lethargy. Caffeine destroys the effects of B-complex vitamins and vitamin C, overstimulates the nervous system, and inhibits the absorption of iron, potassium, silicon, and other trace minerals. Alcohol destroys B and C vitamins and puts sugar into the body system. Smoking should be avoided because of the many health hazards it poses. Foods high in calories and cholesterol contribute to obesity, diabetes, high blood pressure, and heart disease.

Proper nutrition enhances feelings of vigor and overall well-being. Older adults who are providing their bodies with the proper nutrients feel healthy, alert, energetic, vibrant, and alive. They have fewer problems with digestion and with their stomachs. They are less likely to be plagued by headaches and the "sugar blues" and less likely to be tense and unable to sleep from too much caffeine. Eating right contributes to weight control and good muscle tone, enhancing body image and increasing feelings of attractiveness and positive self-concept. Older adults should be encouraged to develop good eating habits.

Keeping Fit Reduces Risk. Regular physical exercise is a major component of physical fitness and good physical health. Exercise, called the only antiaging formula, keeps older adults looking and feeling years younger. It increases muscle strength and flexibility of joints, improves balance and coordination, and contributes to speed and agility. Cardiovascular fitness improves, reducing the risk of heart and lung diseases. Exercises burns up excess sugars and fats and helps the older person to maintain a healthy body weight, in turn diminishing the risk of obesity and diabetes. The positive effects of exercise on the immune system include improved resistance to infections, such as pneumonia and influenza. Exercise also reduces the risk of hypertension and osteoporosis.

Good mental health is a further result of exercise for older people. Through exercise, they release excess energy and tension that might otherwise surface in anxiety or anger. As they concentrate on exercise, they divert the mind from everyday problems. Because exercise results in the release of endorphins, natural opiates produced by the brain, into the bloodstream to produce a natural "high," older adults who exercise regularly feel less tense and anxious. They feel good about themselves and their bodies. They are happier, calmer, and more peaceful and have a greater zest for life.

A healthy body is an asset at any age and particularly in later life when illness and death are more likely. The older person in good physical shape feels safer and more secure by being physically able to escape from danger to accomplish normal tasks. Physically fit elders climb stairs easily, do housework and gardening with ease, enjoy social activities such as dancing, and experience more satisfying sexual performance. Posture and appearance are improved, as is the quality of sleep. Maintaining a high level of physical fitness permits one to travel, engage in favorite leisure pursuits, and visit friends and relatives. Regular exercisers are less likely to suffer from tension headaches, muscle pains, backaches, and neck aches. For all of these reasons, exercise enhances self-esteem and life satisfaction and is important in protecting against depression and suicide.

Walking briskly, swimming, bicycling, and gardening are good exercises for older adults. Running and jogging are not. Exercise should be done regularly, preceded by warm-up stretching and slow exercises and followed by cooling-down exercises and stretching. Starting slowly and gradually increasing exercise time and difficulty is recommended; exercising to the point of exhaustion or pain is to be avoided. It is best to wait two hours after eating to exercise.

Keeping Stress in Check. One important aspect of good physical health is stress management. As Marv Miller (1979) points out, the inability to cope with stress is a major factor in later-life suicide. Good nutrition and regular physical exercise help prepare for the stresses of aging. Older people who have experienced loving parents and a healthy home life, have had good educational and job opportunities, and have enjoyed higher levels of income and a better standard of living in their adult years are better prepared to cope with later-life stress. Those who have negotiated life's problems as young people and middle-aged adults will be better copers in old age.

Eating right and exercising regularly help older individuals manage stress, as do a number of other steps: listening to soft, relaxing music; taking nature walks and spending time outside in the fresh air and sunshine; escaping from tensions through reading, creative activities, fantasy, and daydreaming; and engaging in favorite leisure activities alone or with friends. Particularly relaxing are swimming, sitting in the sauna or a whirlpool bath, and taking long bubble baths. Prayer, meditation, tai chi, yoga, deep breathing, and other relaxation exercises help to lower blood pressure and decrease heart and respiration rate, reduce oxygen consumption, and produce different brain wave patterns and endorphins—all signs of relaxation.

Older adults who get sound sleep are better prepared to cope with the day. Taking short breaks during the day aids in tension reduction and stress management. So does setting a steady pace in doing activities.

The use of imagination and positive imaging should not be overlooked. A French pharmacist, Emil Coué, wrote about the power of the imagination in reducing stress and fighting physical disease and illness and advocated that people repeat the following phrase everyday: "Every day in every way I am getting better and better." Positive imaging and verbalization can actually make people feel better, basically by sending positive messages to the body's immune system and stimulating the production of endorphins. Carl Jung used a healing technique he called "active imagination" in which patients were encouraged to focus on mental images and to communicate with them.

More recently, positive imaging and visualization have been advocated by Bernard Siegel (1986) and others as an effective way to fight disease, especially cancer. Cancer patients are encouraged to visualize their cancer in a particular form, such as the form of a fish, and then to visualize an eating-away process, such as a big shark's eating away all the fish. Patients are taught to see themselves as healthy and free of cancer.

Visualization may be used to help one relax. An older individual who focuses on pleasant thoughts and images and visualizes a quiet, peaceful, beautiful place, perhaps in the mountains or near the ocean, can see in the mind's eye all the sights, smell all the smells, hear all the sounds, and touch all the textures in that serene place. Guided imagery is a positive and relaxing experience and provides a comfortable way to erase tensions. Deep breathing techniques and soothing music can enhance the visualization experience.

Humans' capacity for imagining can lift them from drab and difficult reality to the beautiful world of fantasy and daydreams. The mind becomes a playground for seeing new sights, traveling to distant places, experiencing new emotions, and having fun. In the playground of the mind, physical pain and disabilities disapppear, poverty and problems vanish, and time stands still. Putting aside, even temporarily, the stresses and strains of daily living can be as easy as closing one's eyes and imagining. I am not advocating escapism for older people but rather a temporary relief from pressures and tensions.

Herbert Benson (1975) has described the many benefits of achieving what he calls the relaxation response. Physiological changes that occur when the relaxation response is achieved include a decreased heart and respiraton rate, lowered blood pressure, lowered rate of metabolism, lowered level of oxygen consumption, changes in the immune system, and altered brain wave patterns. These changes are associated with what has been called an altered state of consciousness. A person experiencing the relaxation response feels an intense sense of inner peace, serenity, calmness, selflessness, ecstasy, and unity with a higher being or higher power. After experiencing the altered state of consciousness Benson described, individuals note subjective feelings of well-being and happiness, peace of mind, and a feeling of rising above ordinary problems.

The relaxation response may be achieved by engaging in deep prayer, meditation, or deep relaxation. One way to enter a state of deep relaxation involves intense concentration on breathing, combined with progressive tensing and relaxing of each muscle group from head to toe. The individual takes several deep breaths, focusing on the inhalation and exhalation of air and giving self-messages to relax as air is exhaled. After taking repeated deep breaths in and out and focusing on the flow of air and on relaxing, the individual tenses and then relaxes each muscle group beginning with facial muscles—for example, tensing certain muscles, closing the eyes tightly, pursing the lips, and frowning, and then the self-command to relax the tense muscles is given. The exercise is repeated for muscles in the neck and shoulders, arms, chest and stomach, lower back, thighs and calves, and feet. To be effective, the exercise demands intense concentration.

Social Health

Like people of all ages, older adults need other people to lead a complete and enriching life. Participation in various groups, particularly family, is essential to positive mental health. Older adults, however, have lost many people they love—spouse, children, and close friends. Faced with these deep personal losses, the need for maintaining social ties and social relationships assumes even greater significance in later life.

Social bonds may be provided through involvement in family activities, church and religious groups and activities, or participation in various social groups and activities, particularly with those of similar age. Senior centers, golden age clubs, age-segregated retirement communities, and other social groups for seniors encourage friendship formation and social participation. By communicating with others, older adults achieve a sense of meaning or purpose, develop a sense of personal identity, find emotional support, and combat feelings of isolation, loneliness, and depression. They can find new friends to replace those they have lost and new roles to replace former roles in work and family. They can develop leisure interests and skills and continue to grow intellectually and emotionally.

Human beings have a biological need for touch; it is an actual skin hunger that can be met only by physical contact with another human being. Touch is the earliest sense developed in newborn infants; those who are deprived of physical contact die. Touch is a major form of communication. Through physical touching, individuals develop a healthy sexual identity, bond with others, experience self-awareness and self-love, explore their environment, and experience pleasant sensations. The frequency of touch has an effect on metabolism, the endocrine and muscular systems, and intestinal motility.

Many older adults are deprived of physical contact with others and as a result suffer from a lack of physical stimulation. Their self-esteem and self-concept suffer; they may develop a negative body image from sensual deprivation; and some may come to see themselves as unlovely and unlovable. Touch deprivation creates a sense of alienation from self and isolation from others. These feelings may be experienced as boredom or a lack of energy and being disconnected from other people and the world as a whole.

Therapeutic touch has been used in various civilizations through the ages as a way of healing. The oldest documentation of the healing powers of touch was a classical work in internal medicine from the Orient, *The Huang Ti Nei Ching,* written 5,000 years ago. Hippocrates described the healing powers of touch in his medical writings. Faith healing involves the laying on of hands. More recently, scientific studies of the use of therapeutic touch with heart patients and pain patients show that touch can speed recovery and reduce physical pain.

Older adults who participate actively in family, religious, social, and community activities are more likely to experience touching and all the positive benefits of physical contact. Two beneficial sources of touching are hugging and massage. Massage can be done by another or accomplished by "self-massage." To do a self-massage, tennis balls can be rolled over various parts of the body, a rolling pin can be rolled under the feet, or a brush can be used to stimulate the bottom of the feet, head, or other parts of the body. Back rubs and foot massages are particular favorites of older adults and can be practiced with a partner.

Emotional Health

Older individuals who are emotionally healthy are better prepared to meet the challenges of aging. They have a positive self-concept and high level of self-esteem, they feel good about themselves and their own skills and abilities. They feel confident, secure, and in control of their own life, with a strong sense of who they are and where they are going. Emotionally healthy adults are able to face the stresses of aging and adjust their behavior and life-styles. They are positive, optimistic, and happy and view life as a great adventure or an exciting journey. Obstacles are considered not as problems or crises but as challenges to be mastered. Emotionally healthy older adults are always in the process of becoming; they do not feel they have "arrived." They retain a natural sense of curiosity, awe, and wonder. Life never loses its magic for them. They are open, receptive, spontaneous, playful, and creative. Emotionally healthy individuals can face reality squarely. They live in the present and appreciate the present moment. Another characteristic many emotionally healthy individuals possess is a good sense of humor and the ability to laugh.

Siegel's exceptional cancer patients, who survived despite the odds, retained an optimism and positive outlook on life. In his book, *Most of All They Taught Me Happiness,* Robert Müller (1978) makes a strong case for optimism as a protective, life-giving force. He suggests that individuals choose their own emotions and perspectives on life, they can decide to be happy and optimistic and feel good about themselves. Each day people choose whether they will appreciate life and meet the world with a feeling of zest and joy or despair and see the world as an ugly, frightening place. He believes in the power of auto-suggestion. An individual who thinks positive thoughts and tells the self he or she is happy and healthy will indeed feel healthy and happy and see life, events, and people in a positive way. Müller himself prefers to live on the sunny side of life and offers numerous examples of how such an optimistic outlook has personally served him well in meeting many challenges, including an escape from Nazi soldiers and later successfully enduring imprisonment. His philosophy is best expressed in this passage:

> Like my friend's wife, I "decided" to stop loving nature and to dislike it instead. Forthwith, the beautiful Hudson River became an unnecessary, ugly mass of wasteful water, eternally and boringly renewed for no intelligible purpose. The trees turned into senseless, grotesque parasols fighting in the air with their leaves for a little solar energy and in the ground with their roots for some moisture and chemical nutrients, again for no recognizable purpose. The flowers seemed vain, the crows were killers, the squirrels were vicious, my dreams were illusions, my joy was childish, my job was senseless, my entire life was a wastebasket filled with despair, hopelessness, and death at the end. The more I let the wheels of this new mood unravel its abyss of mud, the more darkness, pestilence, and venom upwelled. I soon felt like

vomiting at life, and it suddenly struck me how easy it was to call forth the specter of suicide. I stopped quickly, awed by the forces I had unleashed in myself. Emerging from this dreadful experience and shaking off its last ugly images, I found myself once more confirmed in my old, intuitive belief, which had guided me all my life—namely, that only one recipe can solve man's problems on his little planet and perhaps on other planets as well: the indomitable will for life, the law of voluntary, determined, conscious love for life and for the world. (p. 203)

Older individuals who see life as a precious gift and appreciate the beauty of the world are protected from depression and suicide. Their happiness can lift them out of the depths of depair and overcome sickness, sadness, poverty, injustice, and imprisonment. Müller calls happiness the "triumph of life; pessimism is its defeat" (p. 209).

Living Creatively. Carl Rogers (1961), in his description of the mature person, emphasized spontaneity and receptiveness to new experiences. Maslow (1962) too noted the strong connection between creativity and what he called self-actualization. The self-actualized—those living to their full potential—demonstrate spontaneity and a freshness of appreciation; they have the awe and wonder of children, an unspoiled creativity, and experience each moment as exciting and new. They are able to distance themselves from a situation and to see novel relationships and creative solutions to problems. Creativity was also one of the characteristics Siegel (1986) discovered in his cancer patient subjects who survived against low odds. Survivors, as he calls them, are curious, have an active imagination, and spend time daydreaming and fantasizing; they are open and receptive. Caroline Bird (1983), in her description of the ageless—individuals who remain young into their later years—found one common characteristic: those who never seem to grow old remain curious and eager to try new things in life. Life for them is an exciting journey. Traveling to exotic places, learning the newest computer technology, and meeting new people occupies their time. They see the world they live in as a magical place with much to offer, many opportunities to be explored, and many exciting things to experience.

Ulysses, the hero of the classical Greek world who was in his 70s when he began his last set of adventures on the high seas, represents the epitome of the creative adventurer of late life. As he calls his comrades together, Ulysses, in the words of Tennyson, gives the following speech:

Come, my friends,
'Tis not too late to seek a newer world.
Push off, and sitting well in order smite
The sounding furrows; for my purpose holds
To sail beyond the sunset, and the baths
Of all the western stars, until I die.
· ·
Tho' much is taken much abides; and tho'
We are not now that strength which in old days
Moved earth and heaven; that which we are, we are;
One equal temper of heroic hearts
Made weak by time and fate, but strong in will
To strive, to seek, to find, and not to yield.

In his book *The Ulyssean Adult,* John McLeish (1976) describes the older adult who, like Ulysses, lives life creatively, pursuing one exciting adventure after another. Ulyssean adults have a sense of quest. They demonstrate courage and resourcefulness. They are not afraid to take risks, to fail, and to make mistakes. They creatively engage in hobbies, other leisure pursuits, arts activities, and living— "drinking life to the lees," as Tennyson's Ulysses puts it. They continue to grow and develop, to sense and to explore, to learn. McLeish describes them in this way:

These Ulyssean people have one thing in common—they are all seekers, and this is reflected in the trajectory of their lives. Some are chiefly thinkers and readers, adventurers in ideas, some chiefly doers, many are both; all are in pursuit of new enterprises for the mind, the body, or the spirit. The scale of the enterprises, whether large or small, is incidental; the symbol of the Ulyssean is the prow of the ship in which Ulysses and his comrades had so many encounters on the swift-running seas. The thrust is outward—ever inquiring, searching, dreaming, growing—outward not downward. (p. 155)

In developing his concept, McLeish said the Ulyssean life is possible for older individuals because in many ways the conditions required for the creative life are more available in the later years: time to rest and to think, a rich storehouse of experiences accumulated through life, and a freedom to adapt unorthodox concepts, one of the recognized patterns of creativity.

Creativity and creative expression can be stimulated and nurtured in older adults through involvement in arts activities. Dance, drama, music, and art have been a vital part of human existence since the earliest attempts to placate the gods with primitive dance around the fire. The use of dance, song, drama, and visual arts in religious and magical ways to cure physical or emotional ills is probably as old as art itself. Primitive tribes used elaborate artistic cures for physical and emotional disorders or to exorcise demons. Aristotle recognized the value of dramatic play for relaxation "as a medicine." Greek tragedies encouraged the expression of such emotions as pity and fear as the actors identified with characters.

Influenced by Sigmund Freud's work, Ernst Kriss (1952) formulated a psychology of creativity, claiming that the process of creating gives the individual the opportunity to harness images and intrapsychic energy into a concrete manifestation. Similarly, Edith Kramer (1958) argues that art is healing because it provides the individual a medium through which to capture and express hidden feelings, thoughts, and impulses. Alfred Adler (1932), who also believed in the therapeutic properties of the creative arts, developed the idea of the creative self, postulating that humans are always in the process of "creative becoming." Involvement in creative activities provides the opportunity to discover interests, to self-actualize, and to choose a posture toward life. Carl Jung (1971) regarded imagination and creativity as healing forces; he felt that deep-seated feelings could be symbolically represented and cathartically released through the creative act that is basically nonrational.

The arts allow for creative expression, development of personal insight, and self-awareness. Similarly, spontaneity, flexibility, and originality resulting from the creative process are encouraged through the use of creative therapies. Art—whether in music, visual media, drama, or dance—is naturally therapeutic. It is a means of expanding the consciousness, of naturally becoming more aware of one's self, particularly of the connection between mind and body. It forces us to become more in tune with our senses and with our bodies. As creative expression, art provides a healthy, natural outlet for feelings and emotions such as fear, doubt, guilt, and grief that plague many older people, and it provides a positive experience of participation in a social group, with accompanying feelings of acceptance and belonging, self-esteem and self-concept, and personal competence, mastery, and accomplishment.

The search for identity—one's sense of who one is and where one stands in relation to God, the universe, and other humans—has always led to music, art, and drama. As Nellie Arnold (1976) expresses it, "The need for self-relation, direction, and life enhancement drives people to search for individuality . . . rather than to remain a part of the mass society." Nowhere can one find a better opportunity to develop and to express individuality and identity than through participation in drawing, painting, sculpting, music, drama, or dance.

Older adults who suffer physical, cognitive, social, and economic losses often come to view themselves as progressively physically and mentally handicapped, declining and dependent. Their self-esteem may plummet, and individuality and independence become increasingly difficult to achieve in later life. Creative arts provide one way to meet the challenges of aging. They offer the older adult a choice, which builds pride, confidence, self-esteem, and a sense of control to offset the negative psychological effects of losses.

Creative arts spark the imagination and transport the older individual to a magical world of symbols and images. In that fantasy world, problems can be solved in creative and imaginative ways. The experience equips the older person to deal creatively with the real problems of later life. Through participating in creating activities, older adults come to view themselves as active, vital, useful human beings.

The arts are inspirational, infusing older adults with a spirit of zest and a liberation in spirit from poverty, pain, and loneliness. They are lifted out of the doldrums of depression when they find creative powers in themselves. The role of creative arts activities is significant as a potential contributor to life satisfaction and psychological health for the elderly.

Laughter and Humor. The merits of laughter and a good sense of humor have been extolled throughout history. In the old Testament we read that "a merry heart doeth good like a medicine" (Proverbs 17:22). The medieval practice of keeping court jesters attests to the value placed on humor by royalty. In *Anatomy of Melancholy,* Robert Burton (1927), an English scholar writing 400 years ago, attributed curative properties to mirth, recognized as the chief engine for alleviating melancholia. Many native American tribes also had ceremonial clowns to entertain. Sigmund Freud considered humor the highest-level defense mechanism and linked humor with the will to live. Freud asserted that laughter saves psychic energy otehwise needed to suppress unacceptable sexual and hostile feelings. The existential philosopher Friedrich Nietzsche recognized the value of laughter when he wrote, "Man alone suffers so excruciatingly in the world that he was compelled to invent laughter."

In a longitudinal study of 268 Harvard University graduates that followed the subjects over a thirty-year period, psychologist George Valliant (1977) identified humor as one of the best defense mechanisms used by mature adults to deal with the strains and tensions of life.

More recently, Norman Cousins (1979), the former editor of the *Saturday Review,* popularized the benefits of humor and laughter in fighting disease and illness. When he returned from an exhausting trip to the Soviet Union in 1964, Cousins was diagnosed as having a serious collagen disease that was causing the connective tissue in his spine and joints to disintegrate. The disease caused excruciating pain, and he was given a one in five hundred chance of fully recovering. Cousins refused to accept that prognosis and, with the help of his physician, took charge of his own recovery program.

Cousins checked out of the hospital and into a motel. He ate a healthy diet, took large doses of vitamin C intramuscularly and put himself on a program of "humor therapy," watching "Candid Camera" episodes and old Marx Brothers' films and reading jokes and humorous books and stories. He laughed a lot and found that the laughter had an anesthetic effect, allowing him to receive pain-free sleep: ten minutes of good belly laughter provided two hours of pain-free sleep. Miraculously, the connective tissue in his joints regenerated. Cousins attributed his recovery in large part to his humor therapy. He was convinced that the positive images he focused on and the humor and laughter had a positive effect on his immune system, which then fought off the progressive disease. Pain was reduced as humor and laughter stimulated the production of endorphins, natural opiates.

Much anecdotal evidence exists that suggests that clowns have a therapeutic effect on hospital patients of all ages (Moody, 1978). Clowns lift the spirits and produce peals of laughter with their antics, and they can be the stimulus for recovery from serious physical illnesses. Siegel (1986) found that cancer patients with a survivor personality are willing to look foolish, make mistakes, and laugh at themselves.

Older adults can derive many psychological and physiological benefits from humor and laughter. Laughter, one of the best ways to release anger, tension, and anxiety and to relax, is an important stress-reduction mechanism. Humor is related to positive self-concept and self-esteem; people who feel good about themselves can laugh at themselves. Laughter and humor can lift the spirits and liberate older people from their troubles and depression. Individuals who laugh and see the humor in life events, in their own mistakes and shortcomings, and in others have a realistic appreciation of the imperfect world we live in and the imperfect people we share our space with. Life becomes less serious and somber. Humor lightens the burdens of living. Humor also brings people together and serves as a positive means of communication.

In addition to these psychological benefits, humor and laughter have physiological benefits. Cousins called laughter a form of "jogging the innards"—it actually exercises the heart, lungs, and other vital organs. Laughter increases the flow of air through the lungs and increases the level of oxygen in the blood. It stimulates the production of catecholamines, which stimulate production of endorphins that enhance feelings of well-being and pain tolerance. Laughter has an anesthetic effect, relieving pain resulting from muscle tension. Laughter increases the heart and respiration rate, enhances metabolism, improves muscle tone, stimulates the immune system, and increases resistance to disease. For all of these reasons, it is important to encourage humor and laughter in the depressed elderly. Jokes, cartoons, and funny stories can serve the purpose, but a sense of humor about life in general is best.

Spiritual Health

The spiritual dimension of health and wellness is uniquely human. By being able to detach oneself from certain situations and from self, one can choose one's own attitude about the situation, self, and life in general. Only people have the ability to rise about their own situation and personal suffering. The meaning of life, love, conscience, hope, courage, and the will to live are all part of the spiritual dimension.

Finding Meaning in Life. Meaning in life is essential, as Albert Einstein noted: "The man who regards his life as meaningless is not merely unhappy but hardly fit for life." Viktor Frankl (1959), a psychiatrist who survived the Nazi death camps, believes the guiding principle in human life is the will to meaning. Frankl and others who survived the Holocaust say they were able to transcend their current situations and suffering mentally and retain a higher meaning and purpose in life. For Frankl, it was his vision of his wife and family and his picture of himself one day lecturing to large audiences about his new version of psychotherapy. Frankl chose to survive and to find meaning in even his intense suffering. He viewed the experience as a way to prepare him for his later work as a psychiatrist. He was able to retain a deep love for his wife, though he did not know if she were still alive, and never lost his appreciation for a beautiful sunset, the majestic Alps, birds, and nature. By using mental imagery Frankl was able to escape from his misery into pleasant surroundings where he could walk and talk with his beloved wife. Frankl was an adherent of Nietzsche's philosophy that "he who has a 'why' to live can bear almost any 'how.'"

In his book, *Man's Search for Meaning,* Frankl (1959) argues that most forms of mental illness result from an existential vacuum. An individual who sees no personal meaning in life is living in an existential vacuum. When nothing is important, nothing is worth working for or fighting for; life becomes boring and meaningless, and individuals become apathetic. What Frankl called an existential vacuum Paul Tillich (1952) referred to as the "anxiety of meaninglessness": "anxiety about the loss of an ultimate concern, of a meaning which gives meaning to all meaning" (p. 49).

Many older adults who commit suicide are living in an existential vacuum. Life holds no meaning for them; they feel they have no purpose or direction in life; there are no goals to strive for, nothing worth becoming committed to or living for. Sigmund Freud once wrote that "the moment a man questions the meaning and value of life he is sick."

Frankl (1959) says the meaning of life is unique for each person:

Life ultimately means taking the responsibility to find the right answer to its problems and to fulfill the tasks which it constantly sets for each individual. These tasks, and therefore the meaning of life, differ from man to man, and from moment to moment. Thus is is impossible to define the meaning of life in a general way. Questions about the meaning of life can never be answered by sweeping statements. "Life" does not mean something vague, but something very real and concrete, just as life's tasks are also very real and concrete. They form man's destiny, which is different and unique for each individual. (p. 157)

Erik Erikson (1987) expanded his theory of development to include integrity as a necessity for successful aging. In Erikson's psychological theory of personality development, each life stage is characterized as a balance between opposites. In infancy, the struggle is to develop trust and overcome mistrust; in adolescence, it is to find identity instead of role confusion. In the last stage of life, the basic issue is to achieve a sense of ego integrity rather than despair. Erikson's concept of integrity refers to the meaning and purpose of life. Older adults who can look back over life and view it as meaningful and worthy of having been lived achieve integrity and wisdom at the end of life. Older adults who see mistakes and failures, bad choices, wrong decisions, and a fruitless life, on the other hand, suffer from despair. Most older adults who choose to end their own lives are suffering from despair. In "The Road Not Taken," Robert Frost demonstrates an individual who has accepted life as meaningful and appropriate and has achieved integrity at life's end:

Two roads diverged in a yellow wood,
And sorry I could not travel both
And be one traveler, long I stood
And looked down one as far as I could
To where it bent in the undergrowth;

Then took the other, as just as fair,
And having perhaps the better claim,
Because it was grassy and wanted wear;
Though as for that, the passing there
Had worn them really about the same,

And both that morning equally lay
In leaves no step had trodden black.
Oh, I kept the first for another day!
Yet knowing how way leads on to way,
I doubted if I should ever come back.

I shall be telling this with a sigh
Somewhere ages and ages hence:
Two roads diverged in a wood, and I—
I took the one less traveled by,
And that has made all the difference.

Simone de Beauvoir (1972), who studied aging in many societies of the world, similarly noted the importance of meaning in successful aging: "Old age exposes the failure of our entire civilization. There is only one solution if old age is not to be an absurd parody of our former life, and that is to go on pursuing ends that give our existence meaning—devotion to individuals, to groups, or to causes, social, political, intellectual, or to creative work."

Commitment to a set of values, to ideals and goals, to causes political, religious, or social, and to people is important at any age. In her encounters with pathfinders—people who are extremely happy and well adjusted and have managed to negotiate successfully the crises of life—Gail Sheehy (1981) found that many had what she called "grit." They were fervently committed to someone or something, and they did whatever it took to fulfill their commitments. It is essential that people be committed to something larger than their "convulsive little ego," to use William James's term.

In *Love, Medicine, and Miracles,* Dr. Bernie Siegel (1986) discusses the importance of the spiritual dimension in the survival of cancer patients. Spiritual faith was one of the four faiths identified as essential for recovery from cancer. Siegel's definition of spirituality is contained in the following passage:

I view spirituality as including the belief in some meaning or order in the universe. I view the force behind creation as a loving, intelligent energy. For some, this is labeled God, for others it can be seen simply as a source of healing. From this there comes the ability to find peace, to resolve the apparent contradictions between one's emotions and reality, between internal and external. Spirituality means acceptance of what is (not to be confused with resignation or approval of evil. . . .) Spirituality means the ability to find peace and happiness in an imperfect world, and to feel that one's own personality is imperfect but acceptable. From this peaceful state of mind come both creativity and the ability to love unselfishly, which go hand in hand. Acceptance, faith, forgiveness, peace, and love are the traits that define spirituality for me. These characteristics always appear in those who achieve unexpected healing of serious illness. (pp. 177–178)

Love. The spiritual dimension encompasses the illusive concept of love, through which we can experience the essence of another person. In *Most of All They Taught Me Happiness,* Müller emphasized the importance of love—the key to happiness and an optimistic, positive outlook. An individual who loves life and loves self and others is able to affirm life, appreciate it, and hold it precious. Love enables individuals to see the magic in life and to appreciate all of the beauties of art and nature. In Müller's words:

> Love for life, passion for life, deep gratitude for every moment of it, extending one's heart and brain into eternity and totality, from the fishes and the fowl to the stars, from youth to old age, from the glaciers to the tropics, from the prodigy of birth to the mystery of death, man can indeed partake in all creation if he switches on, deep inside, the will for life, the decision for happiness, the option for love. I have "decided" to love my life, to throw in my gauntlet for it, to believe in it, to find it exalting in every respect, at every moment, from the beginning to the end. (p. 207)

Viktor Frankl credited love for his survival in the Nazi death camps. His deep love for his wife fortified him against the poverty, pain, and brutality of prison life. The pleasant thoughts of his wife and the bond of love they shared with each other sustained him and lifted him out of his drab prison existence into a beautiful place. Frankl also had a deep love for his fellow prisoners, whom he tried to help. He loved nature and God, had a passionate love for life and a strong will to live that no amount of physical pain and torture could extinguish, and even managed to retain a love for the German guards, whom he saw as a part of humanity.

The capacity to love deeply is a characteristic of self-actualized individuals described by Maslow, mature persons identified by Carl

Rogers, and pathfinders studied by Gail Sheehy. Exceptional cancer patients whom Bernie Siegel (1986) worked with had to transcend fear and hate and develop the capacity for deep love to recover. Love is a healing force; experiencing it strengthens the immune system. The emotion of love sends a message to the body. Siegel is convinced that unconditional love is the most powerful known stimulant to the immune system. By the same token, resentment and hate are powerful negative emotions that keep many people physically sick, as well as sad and unhappy.

Hope. Hope is an equally powerful emotion that contributes to life satisfaction and happiness and protects against depression and suicide. Emily Dickinson described hope in this way:

Hope is the thing with feathers
　That perches in the soul,
And sings the tune without the words,
　And never stops at all.

To hope is to believe that a desired outcome is possible and worth working for. It is the opposite of despair and giving up. Even in the worst of human conditions, Frankl never gave up hope that he would survive the prison camp and be reunited with his wife.

Hope is one of the two gifts that Voltaire said heaven gives us to counterbalance the many miseries of life. It is that spiritual force that whispers, "Go on, you can do it," in spite of all objective aspects that suggest it is useless and impossible. Hope sustains those stuck in poverty, is the force behind those who struggle against all odds to attain a college degree and to achieve success, and contributes to the miraculous recovery of terminal cancer patients and those who, like Norman Cousins, suffer from other progressive diseases. It is hope that helps patients who have just had surgery make remarkable recoveries in spite of a poor prognosis.

One of the major factors in later-life suicide is hopelessness. The individual who has no hope, who sees no way to fulfill his or her desires, who sees no way to get out of the current problem, is vulnerable to depression and suicide.

An older individual who has lost the will to live is a prime candidate for suicide. Studies of suicide by institutionalized elders have made that fact abundantly clear. Older adults living in nursing homes who decided they no longer wanted to live did not live. They either succumbed to a debilitating physical illness that took their life or they took their own life. One woman, who had decided she did not want to live to be older than 80, committed suicide shortly after her eightieth birthday. Another who said she no longer had any reason to be alive, "just turned her face to the wall," to use her expression, stopped eating, and died. Frankl reported similar instances in the Nazi death camps in which prisoners died shortly after giving up and losing their will to live. Many died for no apparent physical reason.

To reduce the risk of suicide in older friends, relatives, and patients, it is important to encourage and to nurture the development of positive thinking and optimism, creativity and creative expression, love, hope, courage, and the will to live. These characteristics can be taught.

Societal Measures in Suicide Prevention

Suicide is a serious public health problem in the United States. Deaths by suicide are potentially among the most preventable. The prevention of suicide among the elderly may depend ultimately on societal changes that reduce poverty, improve health care and mental health services, offer flexible retirement policies, improve preretirement preparation, and promote fewer ageist attitudes and practices and more meaningful roles and oppotunities for social involvement by older adults. A public health approach to the problem of suicide in the aged, much like those aimed at reducing smoking and preventing AIDS, should be adopted. Such an approach needs to emphasize public education and reduce the availability of lethal methods such as guns. Education, development and expansion of special services, and limiting access to suicide methods can go a long way in preventing suicide among the elderly.

Education

Education and training are key components of any suicide prevention effort. The target audience to reach includes older adults themselves, family members and friends of older people, and service providers who work regularly with older people. In particular, education should be aimed at physicians, nurses, hospitals attendants, emergency medical technicians, pharmacists, home health workers, physical therapists, occupational therapists, psychologists, psychiatrists, social workers, mental health clinicians, and rehabilitation counselors; the clergy and funeral directors; law enforcement officers and fire prevention specialists; and directors and staff members of nursing homes, adult homes, adult day care centers, and senior centers.

Older people need education in a variety of areas. First, they need to learn more about aging and the aging process. The strengths and assets of older people should be emphasized to dispel many myths and negative stereotypes.

Older individuals need information to help them prepare for the adjustment to retirement. They could benefit from information about how to cope with widowhood and how to grieve. Wellness education can prepare them to achieve optimum mental and physical functioning. Education about proper nutrition, the value of exercise, and how to relax and reduce stress and tension is valuable. Leisure education is essential. Older people need to learn to appreciate and use their many hours of leisure time in useful and meaningful ways. Leisure education could emphasize the development of a set of leisure values and attitudes, as well as training in particular skills. Creative expression and participation in creative activities should be encouraged.

In addition to such general education, older adults also need information about alcoholism, depression, and suicide. They should be made aware not only of the symptoms of alcoholism and depression and of ways to recognize suicidal thoughts and impulses in themselves and others, but also that alcoholism and depression are treatable and that suicide is not the only alternative to their problems. The vulnerable elderly in particular should be educated regarding the help available to them in their community: psychological and mental health services, support groups (for bereavement and other difficulties), and other church, community, and social services.

Ronald Clarke and David Lester (1989) argue in *Suicide: Closing the Exits* for another type of education. In public information campaigns aimed at reducing smoking or AIDS, the harmful effects of particular behaviors are emphasized dramatically. Such an approach to suicide education may be effective in reducing suicide. Clarke and Lester suggest educating older adults and the general public about the negative effects of suicide. One is that many people survive suicide attempts with terrible and permanent disabilities, such as disfigurement from gunshot wounds or jumping, loss of bowel or bladder control, kidney failure from ingestion of drugs, and memory loss from carbon monoxide poisoning. Survivors, moreover, suffer from many difficulties related to the suicide, including guilt, shame, depression, and an increased risk of suicide. Finally, many religions stigmatize suicide, considering it a sin or an immoral act. When suicide is painted as a disgusting act that shows a lack of love and concern for others and has tremendous economic costs to society, older people may be deterred from taking their own lives.

Family members, friends, and relatives of older adults and service providers who work with older people also need to be educated. They need accurate information about aging and about older people that dispels myths.

Many caregivers and professionals who encounter the depressed suicidal elderly lack accurate or comprehensive information about aging and the aged, depression, alcoholism, and suicide. Their professional training needs considerable improvement to understand the elderly and to prevent later-life suicides.

John McIntosh (1987), a psychologist who works with suicidal older adults and also teaches, discusses the necessary components of suicide education in an excellent article, "Suicide: Training and Education Needs with an Emphasis on the Elderly." The first important component of suicide education is the elimination of dangerous and erroneous myths. The next that he suggests is knowledge about high-risk groups in the older population: elderly white males, particularly widowers, elderly alcoholics, depressed elders, those who are living alone and socially isolated, and the recently widowed. Third is accurate identification of clues and warning signs. Concerned family members and friends and those working with older people need to be aware of the verbal, behavioral, syndromatic, and situational clues to suicide. Clues and warning signs of depression and alcoholism, the major syndromes related to suicide in later life, should be the focus of suicide education programs and public information campaigns. McIntosh points to the need for education about how to assess potential lethality as a part of recognizing suicidal risk. That component includes education about the lethality of particular methods, as well as the importance of a suicide plan, availability, accessibility, and specifically of method. The importance of support systems and significant others as a protection from suicide is also the focus of such education.

McIntosh emphasizes the need for educating about how to interact effectively with a suicidal person. Medical students and others attending professional schools lack adequate training in this area. Indirect forms of self-destructive behavior, such as refusing to eat or drink, are important subjects to address, as are the need for education about medical, psychological, social, religious, and community services available to help elderly alcoholics, depressed older people, and those who are suicidal.

The final type of education McIntosh notes is "postvention," or the need to help survivors following someone else's suicide. Until recently, little attention has been given to survivors, who experience anger, guilt, depression, and shame and are often traumatized by finding the suicide victim. Some studies suggest that survivors of suicide may have an increased risk of committing suicide themselves.

Various strategies of education are available. The media—newspaper, radio, television, videos—are important as educational tools, and the population aged 60 years and over is the largest user of the media. Advertising, informational booklets and brochures, signs in appropriate offices, newsletters, and similar materials are an effective way to reduce ageism and inform about depression, alcoholism and suicide.

Public appearances by celebrities and clinicians on talk shows and at churches and synagogues, community groups, public service clubs, resource fairs, and conferences are yet another avenue.

Networking between professionals in health, mental health, aging, and social services is another effective educational technique. These professionals have a responsibility to dispel negative myths about aging and old people.

Curriculum development at every educational level is an important strategy. Education about aging and older adults is essential to combat ageism. Elementary and secondary schools and colleges could offer courses on suicide and alcoholism. Medical, nursing, and other professional schools currently provide only limited education regarding suicide and alcoholism. This situation should be changed to prepare health and mental health professionals for the challenge of dealing with suicidal patients and clients.

Specialized Services

The depressed and suicidal elderly are underserved by mental health professionals and services, as well as by suicide hot-lines and crisis intervention services. Only about 2 percent of all calls to crisis hot-lines are made by people over the age of 60. As a result, the depressed and suicidal elderly often go unrecognized, undetected, and un-helped. Early detection and treatment of depression and suicidal ide-ation is a key to suicide prevention. To accomplish this, it is essential that more screening services and more forms of active outreach be developed. Accurate assessment measures and screening techniques to detect alcoholism, depression, and suicidal intent in older adults is the first proiority. Screening instruments and techniques should be employed by service providers who often come in contact with vul-nerable elders: hospital discharge planners; family practice physi-cians, internists, cardiologists, and specialists in internal medicine; social workers; home health care workers; church centers, and nutri-tion sites.

Aggressive case finding and active outreach can locate and reach lonely, isolated, depressed, alcoholic, suicide-prone older adults. Such persons must be actively sought using tips from doctors, phar-macists, staff of adult day care centers, the clergy, the police, and others. Health departments, welfare offices, social security offices, and geriatric screening programs can provide relevant leads and in-formation. McIntosh, Hubbard, and Santos (1982) suggest estab-lishing separate hot-lines for the elderly, setting up special centers to reach the troubled elderly, using other seniors in a sort of buddy sys-tem to help those who are vulnerable, and establishing community-based outreach programs to find the suicide-prone elderly. In all of these efforts, early detection is a key to suicide prevention. Informa-tion sharing and coordination and referral to appropriate commu-nity resources, agencies, and treatment programs increase the possibility of early treatment and decrease the risk of suicide in older adults. Special groups who are more vulnerable to suicide in later life should be targeted.

Other medical, mental health, and social services needed are well-ness programs that emphasize good nutrition, encourage regular physical exercise, and educate about stress reduction and relaxation methods. Pain clinics would be beneficial to older individuals who suffer from painful conditions.

The need for separate suicide prevention services for older adults or inclusion of elderly counselors and special age-specific counseling and programs in existing suicide prevention centers would aid in suicide prevention. The need for geriatric mental health services of all kinds is great. Geriatric alcoholism services and special hospital wards and detoxification units for older patients are sorely lacking. Bereavement counseling, retirement and widowhood support groups, suicide survivor groups, reminiscence and life review groups, and peer self-help groups also are needed in many communities. Such programs provide needed emotional and social support and allow older people to explore their feelings about important changes in their lives.

Adult day care centers, senior centers, and other programs based on a socialization model could help reduce loneliness and social isolation. Creative arts programs, trips and tours, intergenerational programs of all types, leisure activities, and increased opportunities for volunteering in the Retired Senior Volunteer Program and others should be greatly expanded to provide meaningful roles and activities, increase opportunities for friendship and socialization, and optimize later-life wellness.

Older adults benefit greatly from pet programs. Pets add joy, fun, and zest to an otherwise lonely life. Many researchers have found that the introduction of domestic animals can result in improved physical health, a reduction in loneliness, and an improvement in mood. Pets provide a fuzzy, furry creature to stroke and to love; they offer a means of tactile stimulation and provide unconditional love to those who care for them. Programs that use animals could help older people enjoy life more and aid in reducing the risk of suicide.

Closing the Exits: Limiting Access to Suicide Methods

It is commonly believed that older adults who are suicidal will find a way to commit suicide, no matter what it takes. The truth is that even among older adults, suicide is often an impulsive act. If the method of self-destruction were not easily available, many suicidal elders would not commit the fatal act. Clarke and Lester (1989) argue that "deeply unhappy people could be prevented from killing themselves by closing the exits"—that is, restricting access to lethal agents such as guns as a major suicide prevention strategy. In Malaysia, where almost all brands of pesticides are cheaply and easily available in local grocery stores, the most common mode of suicide is swallowing insecticides. Jumping is more common in San Francisco where the high and barrier-less Golden Gate and Bay bridges are located.

The most common example offered in support of Clarke and Lester's argument is the dramatic reduction of gas suicides and the overall suicide rate following the detoxification of domestic gas in the United Kingdom in the early 1960s. Before then, a common method of suicide in England was by inhaling toxic gas fumes from gas ovens. The switch from toxic coal-gased gas to nonpoisonous natural gas occurred between 1950 and 1960, and the rate of gas suicides and the overall suicide rate declined dramatically every year from 1960 until 1977. The rate of suicide for the elderly alone was halved.

Two of the most popular methods of suicide in America are firearms and ingestion of pills and poisonous substances. To reduce the rate of elderly suicide, it is essential to limit access to and availability of these two methods.

Guns Can Kill You. In a provocative article written more than twenty years ago, Richard Hofstadter (1970), an eminent historian, described America as a gun culture:

> The United States is the only modern industrial urban nation that persists in maintaining a gun culture. It is the only industrial nation in which the possession of rifles, shotguns, and handguns is lawfully prevalent among large members of its population. It is the only such nation that has been impelled in recent years to agonize at length about its own disposition toward violence and to set up a commission to examine it, the only nation so attached to the supposed "right" to bear arms that its laws abet assassins, professional criminals, berserk murderers, and political terrorists at the expense of the orderly population—and yet it remains, and is apparently determined to remain, the most passive of all the major countries in the matter of gun control. (p. 26)

The gun culture is supported by the frontier image and by popular movies, and in America the gun has symbolic value, particularly for men, who are portrayed using guns and who see guns as part of their macho image. There are more privately owned firearms in the United States than in any other Western society. At least half the households in America posesses a firearm, and about one in four owns a handgun. There are more than 100 million guns in private hands, and more than 2 million handguns are sold every year. The United States has more gun deaths every year than any other country in the world. About half of all deaths from firearms are suicides; the United States leads the world in gun use for self-inflicted deaths. Moreover, the percentage of suicides committed using firearms has risen 50 percent since 1960. Guns are the most lethal method of suicide. For those who want to end their lives, guns represent a quick and effective method. Guns are the major method of suicide chosen by older people living outside institutions. According to figures from the National Center for Health Statistics, more than 65 percent of those aged 60 and older use guns to commit suicide. In his study of 301 completed male suicides, Miller found that 85 percent of the suicides used a gun, and 25 percent of these obtained the gun during the month before they committed suicide.

Handguns are the firearm most frequently used to commit suicide. They are easier to use for suicide than rifles or shotguns and are less likely to disfigure, are more often kept loaded and close at hand, and are viewed in our culture as a personal weapon. Older women increasingly are choosing handguns as their method of self-destruction. Males aged 75 and older are a group at particularly high risk for suicide by firearms. In most states handguns can be bought easily, without a waiting period. No mental or criminal checks are run. The salesperson often even loads the bullets into the gun at the counter. Guns are much too easy to obtain in the United States. If the public were exposed to police reports and photographs showing the blood, half-blown-off faces, and scattered body parts at the suicide scene, perhaps it would be easier to convince them that we need stricter gun control.

There is evidence that the availability of guns is a factor in the suicide rate. Markush and Bartolucci (1984) compared the suicide rates of the nine major geographic regions of the United States. Using survey data from the National Opinion Research Center and Gallup polls on the extent of gun ownership in each region, they found that in regions where guns were more readily available, the suicide rate by firearms and the overall suicide rate were higher than in regions where fewer guns were available. David Lester (1987) also has explored the link between the availability of firearms and the suicide rate by analyzing the number of subscriptions to three gun magazines as an indirect indicator of extent of gun ownership. He found that per capita subscription rates to the three magazines were correlated positively to the rate of firearm suicide and the overall suicide rate.

When guns are easily available, they are more often the method of choice for suicidal people. Do limitations on purchasing and ownership of firearms help reduce suicide? I think so. Recent studies conducted by Medoff and Magaddino (1983) and by Lester (1987) confirmed that states with stricter gun control laws, particularly handgun control, have lower rates of firearm suicide and lower total suicide rates than those states with more permissive regulations. Restrictions on purchasing and selling of firearms were particularly important as a way of deterring suicides. Stricter regulations include requiring a permit to purchase or carry guns, long waiting periods, minimum age requirements, reporting of gun sales to police, and criminal and mental checks. Some states have adopted stricter gun control measures and may serve as examples for other states. In Illinois everyone who buys a firearm of any kind must have a firearms owner identification card. There is a three-day waiting period for handguns and a one-day waiting period for long guns. In eight states a permit-to-purchase system is in place. Anyone purchasing a handgun must obtain a permit from the police before the gun transfer takes place. In California and Tennessee, a fifteen-day waiting period is required before a gun can be bought. Massachusetts and New York authorize the police to issue a handgun permit only when the applicant can establish proof of good character and a good reason for owning a handgun. Hawaii, Michigan, Mississippi, and New York require that every handgun be registered with authorities by the owner.

Taking a strong stand, the National Advisory Committee on Criminal Justice Standards and Goals in 1973 recommended that "the manufacture, sale, and private possession of handguns should be prohibited for all persons other than law enforcement and military personnel." One interesting suggestion comes from the U.S. Products Safety Commission, which proposed to classify bullets as "dangerous substances" and to prohibit their sale. Others concerned about the role of guns in violent deaths, argue for methods to reduce the lethality of guns. They make a strong case for less deadly pellet guns and TASERS (stands for "Tom Swift and his Electronic

Rifle"), which fire electrically charged barbed hooks to disable but not kill.

Drugs: A Convenient Way to Die. Another common suicide method among older adults, particularly women, is ingestion of drugs. Older adults in the "young-old" age category (60–64) more often use drugs as their suicide method of choice. Males and the "old old" (75 and older) more often use guns to commit suicide.

Drug overdose is a more available and accessible method of suicide for older people than are some others. Individuals aged 60 and older consume a quarter of all prescription drugs in the United States and are the major consumers of many over-the-counter drugs. Many older adults stockpile pills into what they refer to as their "suicide kit" or "security" for when things get too bad. Older adults who use drugs to end their lives do not have too much trouble gathering a supply of pills. Many request pills from more than one physician and go to several different pharmacies to get the prescriptions filled. Some older adults swap drugs with friends and relatives. Unfortunately, doctors are often all too ready to prescribe pills to older patients.

The U.S. pharmaceutical industry produces more than 10 billion doses of barbiturates every year. Barbiturates, tranquilizers, antidepressant drugs, and analgesics are the most lethal drugs and the ones most often used in self-destruction. Many older adults possess lethal quantities of drugs in their medicine cabinets.

Drugs are a quick, easy, accessible, and often painless method for suicide. When combined with alcohol, the chances that death will occur are increased. The easy availability and accessibility of lethal drugs poses a major problem for suicide prevention.

Australia, which has experienced major changes in prescription of sedatives, offers an example of how the availability of drugs influences suicide rates. Between 1961 and 1967 Australia, saw a dramatic increase in the number of sedative drugs available and the number of sedative drugs prescribed. During that time, consumption of sedatives in Australia more than doubled. The increase was a direct result of a new government pharmaceutical benefits scheme implemented and heavily subsidized by the government during the early 1960s. An analysis of suicides during that same period (Oliver and Hetzel, 1972) showed a marked increase in the number of suicides using barbiturates between 1960 and 1967. The overall suicide rate in Australia also increased dramatically between 1960 and 1967. In response to rising public concern about the use of those drugs in self-poisoning, the government in 1967 placed severe restrictions on subsidized prescriptions of sedatives. Since 1967 there has been a marked decrease in the availability of and consumption of sedatives. The rate of suicide due to drug ingestion has dropped markedly since 1967, without a concomitant increase in suicide by other means. The Australian experience lends support to the argument that closing the exits is a major way to prevent suicides.

Given the relationship between the availability of drugs and suicide, some changes in the manufacture, prescription, and dispensing of such agents is necessary to reduce the rate of suicide in older adults. At the manufacturing level, the federal government could prohibit or severely limit the type and amount of drugs manufactured. If particularly dangerous drugs are not on the market, they could not be prescribed by physicians or used by patients to commit suicide. Another safety measure would be to manufacture potentially dangerous drugs and package them in individually wrapped foil or plastic blister packs so that each pill would have to be individually unwrapped. Pharmaceutical companies have a responsibility to conduct research to discover less lethal drugs that are equally effective therapeutic agents.

At the prescription level, physicians are the primary players. There is an urgent need to educate physicians about the increased vulnerability of older adults to suicide. In particular, physicians need information about the role of prescription drugs in elderly suicide, especially of older women, and the dangers of particular drugs and alternative drugs that are equally effective but less dangerous.

The government could intervene at the prescibing level—for example, by forbidding the prescription of barbiturates except for hospitalized patients or those who need them on a maintenance basis to control seizures. Certainly cancer patients and other terminally ill patients who are suffering intense pain should be able to benefit from such drugs.

Some simple prescribing policies could help reduce the risk of suicide. First, physicians should prescribe any drugs that could potentially be used for self-destruction in small quantities with no refills to limit the available supply. Second, potentially dangerous drugs should be prescribed in suppositories rather than oral tablets.

Would-be suicides are not likely to overdose using suppositories. Third, physicians should prescribe drugs that pose the least risk for suicide. For example, the antidepressant Tolvon seems to be a much safer antidepressant than some others currently prescribed. Tolvon is much less toxic than many other antidepressants when taken in large quantities. Nonbarbiturates should be used where available. Finally, physicians should never prescribe potentially dangerous drugs over the telephone. A personal visit to the physician should be mandatory.

At the point of dispensation, the pharmacist is the key player. Like physicians, pharmacists need to be educated about the increased risk of suicide in older people and about the role of drugs in elderly suicide. They must be aware of individuals who appear to be filling an unusual number of prescriptions from different doctors for drugs that can be used to commit suicide. Drug monitoring systems and increased involvement of pharmacists in drug monitoring would be helpful.

Computer drug utilization review programs are a new dimension in monitoring drug prescription and consumption. These systems have been used in institutions and in the community to identify patterns of drug prescription and drug use in residents of institutions, community pharmacy clients, and outpatients in health maintenance organizations and medical clinics. Such systems are in place in California, South Carolina, and Massachusetts. In a computerized system, the pharmacist enters each new drug into the patient's profile at a computer terminal. The profile displays patient status information (e.g., Medicaid) and information on the interaction potential of the prescribed drug. The patient's drug history is displayed, including dates of all drug renewals and a brief sequence on characteristics and use of all other drugs. A warning of potential drug-drug interaction of the new prescription and any other drugs the patient is currently taking is displayed. Patients filling a number of prescriptions of potentially lethal drugs can be identified instantly. The pharmacist can call the patient's physician and report his or her concerns. Since older adults may fill prescriptions at different pharmacies, a central registry of information accessible by all local pharmacists with access to a computer terminal should be put into place across the country.

A public health approach to suicide prevention emphasizes education and informational campaigns. Another main plank of such an approach is to make it more difficult for those who wish to take their own lives to obtain the lethal means to do so.

8

The Right to Die: Is It Right?

On June 4, 1990, 54-year-old Janet Adkins ended her life lying on a cot in the back of a Volkswagen van parked in a Michigan suburb. Aided by a retired pathologist, Dr. Jack Kevorkian, Adkins was hooked up to his homemade "suicide machine." She had a needle inserted in her arm, which first started saline flowing and, then, when she pressed the button on the macabre death machine, sent first a sedative and then deadly potassium chloride flowing into her veins.

An active woman with loving children and grandchildren, Adkins had flown 2,000 miles from her Oregon home to Michigan to seek Kevorkian's assistance in ending her life when she was diagnosed with Alzheimer's disease. Adkins was an active member of the Hemlock Society, an organization that supports legalizing assisted suicide in America. She made a deliberate decision to end her life rather than face the mental decline associated with senile dementia. Kevorkian, a long-time proponent of physician-assisted suicide, took that opportunity to use his suicide machine as a way of making a public statement to the medical community and the larger society that suicide is acceptable and that doctors should be willing to assist those who choose to die. Kevorkian was not charged with any crime, although a temporary restraining order was issued forbidding him to use his suicide machine again. Ignoring the order, Kevorkian helped two other women to kill themsleves in October 1991. He has recently been charged with first-degree murder.

Two months after Janet Adkins committed suicide using Dr. Kevorkian's suicide machine, another woman, also a member of the Hemlock Society, flew to Michigan, where she also ended her life with the assistance of her husband and daughter. Virginia Harper, 69, who was diagnosed with breast cancer in 1983, was so ill and in

141

so much pain that in August 1990 she asked her husband, Robert, and her daughter, Shanda, to accompany her to Michigan and ensure that her suicide would be successful. She had tried unsuccessfully to commit suicide in 1989.

Harper had read the news reports about Adkins's suicide with Kevorkian's aid. Knowing that no formal charges were brought against Kevorkian in Michigan, Harper decided that it would be safer for her family members to assist her to commit suicide in that state. The Harpers flew to Michigan, where they checked into a Comfort Inn on the outskirts of Detroit. Two hours later Virginia Harper wrote a suicide note indicating that she had asked her husband and daughter to be with her. She took ten Dalmane and a small amount of dramamine and slipped a plastic bag over her head to ensure her death. The pills did not send her into a deep sleep but made her feel hot and uncomfortable. She took the plastic bag off her head. Her husband put the bag back on her head and pulled the elastic bands tight around his wife's neck. She died shortly after. Robert Harper reported her death. He was charged by the district attorney's office with first-degree murder. Mr. Harper has recently been acquitted.

These two cases have brought dramatically to the nation's attention the debate over the right to die with dignity and the ethics of helping others to commit suicide. Suicide and assisted suicide are issues particularly relevant to older members of our society. Dramatic medical advances have greatly increased life expectancy but also have increased the period of chronic illness and disability. A growing population of older citizens places considerably greater financial and social demands on society. The rapid rate of cultural change, resulting in a situation in which older people may have outlived their previous roles and sources of value and meaning, has spawned moral and ethical dilemmas about suicide and assisted suicide among the old.

Today the issues of suicide and assisted suicide are hotly debated among religious leaders, politicians, and older adults. Related issues of health care cost-containment and age-based rationing of health care are also at the forefront of policy discussions.

The Case against Eldercide

Later-life suicide is a tragedy. The fact that we have created a society that is so harsh to its old that ever-increasing numbers are choosing to take their own lives to escape is a sad commentary. Most elders who commit suicide are not suffering intense physical pain or dying from a terminal illness. Rather, they are leading lives of desperation and despair, aching from loneliness, lack of social contact, and rejection and abandonment by a youth-oriented society.

Instead of trying to provide meaningful roles and activities for older citizens, instead of looking for more effective analgesics and pain management strategies and better ways to care for the ill and dying, instead of honoring and respecting elders for their wealth of valuable knowledge and experience and their wisdom, we put forth elaborate arguments about why our old should have the right to commit suicide and to be helped by others to end their lives. Some ethicists, religious leaders, scholars, medical doctors, politicians, and policymakers even go further, arguing that it is in the best interest of society to limit the amount of life-sustaining medical care and technology available to the old.

Masquerading as benevolent protectors who offer many new "rights"—the right to "die with dignity," the right to self-determination, and the right to a "living" will—advocates of suicide, sanctioned assisted suicide, euthanasia, and limited availability of life-prolonging medical technology for the old are promulgating a dangerous new medical ethic that proposes to save money and other resources by letting nonproductive people die or by sanctioning their suicides. We are witnessing the emergence of a medical ethic that says, essentially, "Don't waste scarce time and medical and economic resources on those who would be better off dead." A high value is placed on cost-effectiveness. At the base of this ethic is the same belief that guided Nazi Germany: that some life is not worth living. The view that a person who is no longer useful and productive should be sacrificed or should willingly sacrifice himself or herself so scare resources can be used instead to help the young and healthy endangers older, sicker member of the society. Wide acceptance of such an ideology is unacceptable in affluent America.

An ideology that demands the sacrifice of nonproductive older persons for the benefit of younger, healthier members of society is a barbaric and death-hastening ideology contrary to the Judeo-Christian ethic of humans as a divine creation and human life as a precious gift and a blessing to be cherished and preserved. It is, moreover, contrary to the medical ethic of curing disease, alleviating pain, and preserving life.

Rather than condoning, and even advocating, suicide of the old, we should be doing everything we can to prevent it. We must appreciate the last stage of life as a valuable period with its own unique surprises, special challenges, and opportunities. We must love, honor, and respect the old, who worked to build the society we all live in and now enjoy and who have much of value to give to our children and to us.

This position may appear conservative, even archaic, to some. It flies in the face of well-entrenched, passionately defended social and medical views and values about who should live or die and under what conditions and who makes decisions about life and death. There are many who argue against this position, but their arguments are often unfounded.

To argue for the right to suicide and assisted suicide for the old is a symbol of our devaluation of old age. This position endorses the belief that the answer to the problems of old age is suicide. Moreover, it may in fact be setting up conditions that rob older people of their right to live. Older people, living in a suicide-permissive society characterized by ageism, may come to see themselves as a burden on their families or on society and feel it is incumbent on them to take their own lives. Others may be pressured into suicide by uncaring or greedy family members. Those who need expensive medical technology to live may be denied help and die. The right to die then becomes not a right at all but rather an obligation. We may create a climate in which suicide is viewed as a rational choice. Older people may come to feel it is their social duty to kill themselves.

Suicide is not the only solution for elders suffering from phsyical pain or serious illness. We should be concerned with discovering better painkillers and with properly administering the analgesics currently available. We should devote attention to finding better ways to care for the sick and dying. Human beings can find meaning in and even benefit from their suffering. Survivors of concentration camps, disaster victims, and patients who have recovered from serious illnesses have found great meaning in their suffering and have credited their experiences of pain and illness for making them stronger, more caring, and more capable human beings. We must take care not to rob suffering and dying of existential meaning.

Advocates of the right to die with dignity look to the past to bolster their arguments. The ancient Greek Stoics and Epicureans condoned suicide, especially for the old and those suffering from pain or sickness, and they viewed the choice of one's own death as the ultimate expression of human freedom and the essential component of human dignity. In primitive societies, it was conventional, and occasionally obligatory, for old people to commit suicide or to be assisted in dying if, because of infirmity, they had become a burden on their society. The ancient Scythians regarded suicide as the greatest honor when they became too old for the nomadic life. They had themselves buried alive as soon as age or sickness troubled them (Alvarez, 1972). Among the Yuit of the St. Lawrence Islands in northern Canada, the practice was for an older adult, usually a male, to communicate his wish to die to his family and to seek their assistance. Three methods of execution (assisted suicide) were used: hanging, shooting, and stabbing. The older person was dressed in funeral clothing and carried to the place of destruction, where the execution was carried out in public. The institution served to eliminate members of the society who were diminished by age or sickness and to provide more of the scare resources found in the harsh Arctic climate to younger, more able members of the society (Baqucher, 1979).

Ethicist Daniel Callahan (1987) has called for "a willingness to ask once again how we might creatively and honorable accept aging and death when we become old, and not always struggle to overcome them" (p. 24). In his system of proposed rationing of medical care, sick, old people should be prepared to forego long, expensive (and what he considers will eventually be useless) medical care. The primary orientation and aspirations of the elderly, he believes, should be to the young and to future generations rather than to the advancement of the welfare of their own age group. Moreover, Callahan suggests that the government ration health care to the elderly to meet the needs of all other groups within the society: "Government cannot be expected to bear, without restraint, the growing social and economic costs of health care for the elderly. It must draw lines, because technological advances almost guarantee escalating and unlimited costs which cannot be met, and because in any case it has a responsibility to other age groups and other social needs, not just to the welfare of the elderly." Callahan's argument is a social justice argument for age-based denial of treatment.

In his proposed system, Callahan's primary emphasis in the care of the elderly would be the relief of suffering. The government does have a duty to help people live out a natural life span of about 75 years. Beyond that point, the government should be responsible only for providing the means necessary to relieve undue suffering, so that the individual lives out "a fitting span of life followed by a tolerable death," defined as one that occurs at that point in the life span when "(a) one's life possibilities have on the whole been accomplished, (b) one's moral obligations to those for whom one has had responsibility have been discharged; and (c) one's death will not seem to others an offense to sense or sensibility, or tempt others to despair and rage at the finitude of human existence." Another stipulation about "tolerable death" is that it should not be accompanied by unbearable or degrading pain.

Callahan's argument assumes that aging is synonymous with disease, disability, and loss of function. But the fact is that some older adults are healthy and vital, whereas some younger people (for example, accident victims) are seriously impaired and even in a vegetative state. Rationing of health care is a good idea in itself, but, in light of evidence that many exceptional cases exist, it should be done not on the basis of age but on sound medical grounds.

Nevertheless Callahan has been very influential. Many politicians and policymakers faced with difficult policy issues and voter unrest about escalating health care costs, have read and accepted his views. Certainly as the aging population continues to expand rapidly and we as a nation continue to spend more dollars on health care costs and advanced medical technology, which are disproportionately utilized by the elderly, the need for budget cutting, health care rationing, and redistribution of health and other resources becomes more pressing, and cries for rational suicide, the right to die, and legalized assisted suicide grow louder. It seems easier to eliminate the problem or to encourage it to eliminate itself through suicide than to face hard moral choices about our financial spending as individuals and as a society. Advocates of rational suicide and assisted suicide paint a picture of life and death as rational, orderly, and tidy. But life is not neat and orderly, easily organized and understood. Neither is death.

Easy acceptance of the concept of rational suicide and legalizing of assisted suicide threatens the moral fiber of the country and creates a future society in which suicide is not only expected but even demanded of all who might be a burden. Such a belief system conveniently relieves society of the responsibility to provide a meaningful existence for older or disabled members and to invest in strategies for meeting their physical health care and mental health care needs.

Advocates of the right to suicide and assisted suicide for the old ignore the sanctity of life in the last stages and claim that some lives are not worth living. The sanctity-of-life argument rests on an absolute Judeo-Christian value: the sacredness of life. All life is sacred; the taking of human life, by any means and regardless of the reason, is wrong. Life is a gift from God to be revered.

In the fifth century, St. Augustine condemned suicide as a direct violation of the sixth commandment, "Thou shalt not kill." Eight centuries later, another theologian-philosopher, St. Thomas Aquinas, contended that to commit suicide is to usurp God's power over creation and death and is contrary to the natural human inclination and the law of nature. He condemned suicide as an offense also against the state because it violates the moral obligations an individual has to the community of which he or she is a part.

The program that annihilated more than 6 million people in Germany began by postulating that there is such a thing as life unworthy to be lived. The Nazis initially intended to eliminate only the severely and chronically ill. Eventually those deemed unworthy to live included the socially unproductive, the racially unwanted, the senile, and finally all "useless eaters," figuratively people devoid of value who are taking food from the mouths of those considered worthy (Humphrey and Wickett, 1986, p. 22). They began enforced sterilization of people with hereditary illnesses and the systematic elimination of severely disabled and chronically ill individuals—the mentally impaired, psychotic, epileptic, and victims of infantile paralysis. The program expanded to Parkinson's disease and multiple sclerosis, as well as those suffering from infirmities of old age. These lessons from the past must be guidelines for future policies.

Sanctioning suicide and assisted suicide by the elderly is a threatening symbol of our devaluation of old age and, by extension, life itself. When we view old age as not worth living and old people as less than human, we may not be far removed from our Nazi predecessors.

The ancient Stoics condoned suicide, but they also believed in universal human freedom. Depriving any group of individuals or any person of freedom of choice, whether subtly or overtly, is diametrically opposed to these principles. Many critics of the view that demands the right to suicide point out that while liberty for some may result, others could lose their freedom—older people who would not choose to die willingly but would be pressured into the choice by family members or by society, as well as those who might make an irrational choice for death when they are temporarily in pain, suffering from the toxic effects of disease, or severely depressed or under the influence of drugs or alcohol.

Coercive suicide is yet another possibility. Someone in a position to gain financially could persuade the dying person that suicide is the best choice or make life so unpleasant that the dying person would be inclined in that direction.

Changes in our society's values and beliefs may already be convincing some to accept suicide as rational and the best solution for them. Media presentations, advertisements, and rhetoric from social, religious, and medical professionals may be helping to change the beliefs and values of the culture. The profusion of recent literary accounts favoring suicide and assisted suicide, particularly Derek Humphrey's best-selling *Final Exit,* and increasingly frequent court decisions favoring patients' rights to refuse medical treatment, even when refusal will mean death, may be influencing more older people to choose suicide. In a suicide-permissive society, this choice may appear rational; opting to live might be viewed as selfish, cowardly, or crazy. Are we creating a climate in which suicide is viewed as the rational choice—even a social duty?

The prototype of the elderly suicide is an old man, retired, who has lost his wife and lives alone. He never gets visits from family or friends. He is not actively involved in church, community or other social activities. He is lonely, isolated and depressed. He feels helpless and hopeless and sees no meaning in his present existence. He desperately misses his wife, and also his children, who do not live nearby and who are caught up in their own lives and their own problems. He may turn to alcohol or other drugs to drown his sorrows and escape his loneliness and problems. One day, out of sheer desperation and loneliness, he takes a gun and shoots himself in the head and escapes his meaningless existence. To claim that suicide is a rational choice and the right of every human being plays down the tragedy of late-life suicide.

Most proponents of the right to die and of death with dignity, as well as those who favor rational suicide and legalized assisted suicide for the old, argue from the perspective of terminal illness and pain and suffering. And newspaper accounts and television programs on the topic of elderly suicide selectively portray the suicidal elderly as ill and in intense physical pain. These outspoken advocates and media representatives have mistakenly given the general public the impression that most older people who choose suicide are sick and in pain or are suffering from a terminal illness. The fact is that this is not true. Research studies conducted with cancer patients show that these patients and the terminally ill are not at increased risk of suicide. In a 1984 report, Karolyn Siegel and Peter Tuckel tested the assumption that, regardless of age, persons with cancer commit suicide more frequently than members of the general population. They found that the rate of suicide among cancer patients did not exceed that of the general population and suggested that it is the patient's intrapsychic organization, and not the disease itself, that is the critical factor in determining whether the individual is suicidal.

Avery Weisman (1974) also examined motives for suicide among cancer patients. Based on his work with these individuals, he determined that social dissonance, due to loss of functioning and integration, is more important in decisions to commit suicide than is physical disfigurement and deterioration. He found most significant the fact that the patients who decided to commit suicide felt lonely, isolated, depressed, and without hope.

An individual in a depressed mood lacks the ability to compare suicide with other alternatives to a problem. Depression has another insidious influence: it affects a person's judgment about probabilities. In a gloomy frame of mind, an older depressed person is unable to recall memories that support a less dark prediction. An elderly widower cannot envision life without his wife and, because of the pessimistic self-image related to his depression, cannot accurately remember pleasures he pursued as an individual and the other joys life has offered him in the past. Depression creates tunnel vision. For depressed people, present unpleasant states weigh far more heavily than probable future pleasant ones. The present looms large, the future small and distant. Without the ability to see a better future, present problems may cause an older person to choose suicide. The older adult who has been abusing alcohol or other substances is also incapable of making a rational decision to end his or her life.

But depression—and alcoholism—are treatable conditions. Antidepressant drugs, electroconvulsive therapy, and psychosocial therapies, such as reminiscence therapy, creative arts therapies, family therapy, and individual and group psychotherapy, are effective treatments for later-life depression. Effective treatment of alcoholism in older adults involves detoxification to remove the physical dependence on the chemical; rehabilitation through education, psychotherapy, family therapy, and support group involvement; and follow-up and aftercare, which encourages continuing education and involvement in support groups, as well as personal growth and development and holistic health practices, to remain drug free. More people should advocate for accurate diagnosis and treatment of depression and alcoholism in older people than for the right to commit "rational" suicide. And we as a society have to be willing to pay for treatment and services.

For elders suffering from physical pain or possibly from a terminal illness, there are other solutions besides suicide. We should aim for improved teaching on the care of the dying, more hospices, more medical staff, continued research into the prevention, therapy, and cure of disease, improved pain alleviation methods, and doctors who prescribe sufficient painkillers for terminally ill persons.

Often pain can be effectively controlled without elaborate or expensive outlays. And there is always the possibility that a cure will be found for whatever painful condition afflicts the older person. The number of cancers coming under control in the last two decades is a case in point. Told he was terminally ill, Norman Cousins put himself on a program of exercise and laugh therapy and recovered. How many more, like Norman Cousins, might never have the opportunity to recover if suicide and assisted suicide become widely accepted? As Margaret Pabst Battin (1980) points out, "What sense of duty we have to care for the old and infirm derives in part from our conviction that their regrettable physical condition is inescapable. That sense of duty might flag if we came to see their continued existence as a matter of choice for them" (p. 127).

The survival of the human community rests on the constraint against taking of human life. Where would society be if everyone did it? Where would we stop?

Later Life Is Worth Living

Many people who view suicide and assisted suicide among the old as acceptable fail to see any meaning or value in the last stage of life.

Certainly later life brings many losses and disappointments, as all other stages of human life cycle do, but it also offers challenges and surprises. In the last stage of life, it is possible to find unexpected meaning. Florida Scott-Maxwell, a world traveler and psychotherapist, ended her days in a nursing home. She found herself pleasantly surprised by what advanced old age held for her. In her journal (1968) she wrote:

> We who are old know that age is more than a disability. It is an intense and varied experience, almost beyond our capacity at times, but something to be carried high. . . .
> . . . Though drab outside—wreckage to the eye, mirrors of mortification—inside we flame with a wild life that is almost incommunicable. . . . We have reached a place beyond resignation, a place I had no idea existed until I arrived here. (pp. 5, 6)

It is in later life that maturing forms of hope, will, purpose, competence, fidelity, love, and care are integrated into a comprehensive sense of wisdom. Finally, freed from the pressures of work and responsibilities of family life, one has time to appreciate and enjoy life, look inward, contemplate, and create.

Those who see the end of life as meaningless and even pathetic have a static view of life and of the self. They are unable to conceive of the changing nature of life and of the self. However diminished the body and however changed the life circumstances in later life, the mind and spirit can still flourish. At all stages of life, even as we are sick and dying, we have the capacity to set new goals, redefine the self, and find valid meaning and integrity in our existence.

As a society we can choose to see suicide among the elderly as a rational decision, in the best interest of the individual and the society, or we can see it as a tragedy—in many cases, a preventable tragedy. The poem that follows was written by Dylan Thomas (1914–1953) in celebration of the triumphant life force still present in the old and dying. It tells us that death comes too soon even for those who have arrived at the fullness of their days, and so we may adopt it as a battle cry. Our fight is against the forces that arise not from within, but from societal pressures that are in danger of consigning our elderly to a premature end.

Do not go gentle into that good night,
Old age should burn and rave at close of day;
Rage, rage against the dying of the light.

Though wise men at their end know dark is right,
Because their words had forked no lightning they
Do not go gentle into that good night.
Good men, the last wave by, crying how bright
Their frail deeds might have danced in a green bay,
Rage, rage against the dying of the light.

Wild men who caught and sang the sun in flight,
And learn, too late, they grieved it on its way,
Do not go gentle into that good night.

Grave men, near death, who see with blinding sight
Blind eyes could blaze like meteors and be gay,
Rage, rage against the dying of the light.

And you, my father, there on the sad height,
Curse, bless, me now with your fierce tears, I pray.
Do not go gentle into that good night.
Rage, rage against the dying of the light.

References

Adler, A. 1932. *The practice and theory of individual psychology.* New York: Harcourt Brace.

Alvarez, A. 1972. *The savage god.* New York: Random House.

Arnold, N. 1976. *The interrelated arts in leisure: Perceiving and creating.* St. Louis: Mosby.

Baqucher, J. 1979. *Suicide.* New York: Basic Books.

Battin, M. P. 1980. Manipulated suicide. *Bioethics Quarterly* 2:123–124.

Benson, H. 1975. *The relaxation response.* New York: Morrow.

Bird, C. 1983. The good years: Your future in the 21st century. *Modern Maturity,* April/May, pp. 36–39.

Blazer, D. 1982. *Depression in late life.* St. Louis: Mosby.

Brubaker, T. H., and Michael, C. M. 1987. Amish families in later life. In D. E. Gelfand and C. M. Barresi, eds., *Ethnic dimensions of aging,* pp. 108–117. New York: Springer Publishing Company.

Burton, R. 1927. *The anatomy of melancholy.* New York: Vintage books.

Butler, R. 1975. *Why survive? Being old in America.* New York: Harper & Row.

Callahan, D. 1987. *Setting limits.* New York: Simon and Schuster.

Cary, J. 1942 *To be a pilgrim.* New York: Harper.

Chinen, A. B. 1989. *In the ever after.* Wilmette, Ill.: Chiron Publications.

Clarke, R. V., and Lester, D. 1989. *Suicide: Closing the exits.* New York: Springer Verlag.

Cousins, N. 1979. *Anatomy of an illness.* New York: Bantam Books.

de Beauvoir, S. 1972. *The coming of age.* New York: G. P. Putnam's Sons.

Dunn, H. L. 1961. *High level wellness.* Arlington, Va.: R. W. Beatty, Ltd.

Durkheim, E. 1897/1951. *Suicide.* New York: Free Press.

Dychtwald, K., and Flower, J. 1989. *Age wave: The challenges and opportunities of an aging America.* Los Angeles: Jeremy P. Tarcher.

Emerson, R. W. 1886. Old age. In *Society and solitude: Twelve chapters.* Boston: Houghton Mifflin.

Erikson, E. H., Erikson, J. M., and Kibnick, H. Q. 1987. *Vital involvement in old age.* New York: W. W. Norton.

Farber, M. L. 1968. *Theory of suicide.* New York: Funk & Wagnalls.

Fischer, D. 1977. *Growing old in America.* New York: Oxford University Press.

Frankl, V. 1959. *Man's search for meaning.* Boston: Beacon Press.

Freud, S. 1960. *Jokes and their relation to the unconscious.* New York: W. W. Norton & Company.

Friedan, B. 1963. *The feminine mystique.* New York: Norton.

Gerbner, G. 1961. Press perspectives in world communication: A pilot study. *Journalism Quarterly* 38:312–322.

Goffman, E. 1963. *Stigma: Notes on the management of spoiled identity.* Englewood Cliffs, N.J.: Prentice-Hall.

Hite, S. 1976. *The Hite report.* New York: Dell.

Hofstadter, R. 1970. America as a gun culture. *American Heritage* 21:4–7, 26–34.

Hotchner, A. E. 1966. *Papa Hemingway: A personal memoir.* New York: Random House.

Humphrey, D., and Wickett, A. 1986. *The right to die.* New York: Harper & Row.

Humphries, R., trans. 1958. *The satires of Juvenal.* Bloomington: Indiana University Press.

Jung, C. 1971. *The portable Jung.* Edited by J. Campbell; translated by R. F. C. Hull. New York: The Viking Press.

Kastenbaum, R., and Coppedge, R. 1985. Suicide in later life: A counter trend among the old-old. In G. L. Maddox and E. W. Busse, eds., *Aging: The universal human experience,* pp. 301–308. New York: Springer Publishing.

Kramer, E. 1958. *Art therapy in a children's community.* Springfield, Ill.: Charles C. Thomas.

Kris, E. 1952. *Psychoanalytic explorations in art.* New York: International University Press.

Lester, D. 1987. An availability-acceptability theory of suicide. *Activitas Nervosa Superior* 29:164–166.

Lester, D. 1989. Gun ownership and suicide in the United States. *Psychological Medicine* 19, 519–521.

McIntosh, J. L. 1985. Suicide among the elderly: Levels and trends. *American Journal of Orthopsychiatry* 55:288–293.

McIntosh, J. L. 1987. Suicide: Training and education needs with an emphasis on the elderly. *Gerontology and Geriatrics Education* 7:125–139.

McIntosh, J. L., Hubbard, R. W., and Santos, J. F. 1982. Suicide among the elderly: A review of issues with case studies. *Journal of Gerontological Social Work* 4:63–74.

McLeish, J. A. B. 1976. *The Ulyssean adult: Creativity in the middle and later years.* New York: McGraw-Hill.

Markush, R. E., and Bartolucci, A. 1984. Firearms and suicide in the United States. *Journal of Public Health* 74:123–127.

Maslow, A. 1962. *Toward a psychology of being.* New York: D. Van Nostrand Co.

Masters, W. H., and Johnson, V. 1966. *Human sexual response.* Boston: Little, Brown.

Mather, Cotton. 1716. *The dignity and deity of ancient servants of the Lord.* Boston.

Matthews, S. 1979. *The social world of older women.* Beverly Hills: Sage Publications.

Mayfield, D. G., and Montgomery, D. 1972. Alcoholism, alcohol intoxication, and suicide attempts. *Archives of General Psychiatry* 27:349–353.

Medoff, M. H., & Magaddino, J. P. 1983. Suicides and firearm control laws. *Evaluation Review* 7:357–372.

Menninger, K. 1938. *Man against himself.* New York: Harcourt Brace Jovanovich.

Meyers, J. 1985. *Hemingway: A biography.* New York: Harper & Row.

Miller, M. 1979. *Suicide after sixty: The final alternative.* New York: Springer Press.

Miller, M. 1978. Toward a profile of the older white male suicide. *Gerontologist* 18:80–82.

Moody, R. A. 1978. *Laugh after laugh: The healing power of humor.* Jacksonville, Fla.: Headwaters Press.

Moore, P. 1985. *Disguised.* Albuquerque: Word Books.

Müller, R. 1978. *Most of all, they taught me happiness.* New York: Doubleday.

National Advisory Committee on Criminal Justice Standards and Goals. 1976. *Private security report of the task force on private security.* Washington, D.C.: Law Enforcement Assistance Administration.

Oliver, R. G., and Hetzel, B. S. 1972. Rise and fall of suicide rates in Australia: Relation to sedative availability. *Journal of Australia* 2:919–923.

Osgood, N. J. 1988. *Final report on a study of suicide among the elderly in Virginia.* Submitted to the Virginia Department for the Aging, Richmond.

Osgood, N. J., Brant, B. A., and Lipman, A. 1990. *Suicide among the elderly in long-term care facilities.* Westport, Conn.: Greenwood Press.

Palmore, E. 1975. *The honorable elders: A cross-cultural analysis of aging in Japan.* Durham, N.C.: Duke University Press.

Paton, W. R., ed. and trans. 1916. *The Greek anthology.* 5 vols. Cambridge, Mass.: Harvard University Press.

Pontanus, J. (ed.). 1986. *The metamorphoses* (Ovid). New York: Garland Publications.

Rado, S. 1933. Psychoanalysis of pharmacothymia. *Psychoanalytical Quarterly* 2:1–23.

Rogers, Carl 1961. *On becoming a person.* Boston, Mass.: Houghton Mifflin.

St. Augustine. 1950. *The city of God.* New York: Modern Library.

St. Thomas Aquinas. 1964. *Summa theologiae.* Cambridge: Blackfriars.

Scott-Maxwell, F. P. 1968. *The measure of my days.* New York: Knopf.

Selye, H. 1956. *The stress of life.* New York: McGraw-Hill.

Shahrani, N. (1981). Growing in respect: Aging among the Kirghiz of Afghanistan. In P. T. Amoss and S. van Harrell, eds., *Other ways of growing old: Anthropological perspectives,* pp. 175–191. Stanford, Calif.: Stanford University Press.

Sheehy, G. 1981. *Pathfinders.* New York: William Morrow & Company, Inc.

Shneidman, E. 1985. *Definition of suicide.* New York: John Wiley and Sons.

Siegel, B. S. 1986. *Love, medicine and miracles.* New York: Harper & Row.

Siegel, K., and Tuckel, P. 1984–1985. Rational suicide and the terminally ill cancer patient. *Omega* 14(3):263–269.

Simmons, L. 1945. *The role of the aged in primitive society.* New Haven: Yale University Press.

Steinbeck, J. 1939. *The grapes of wrath.* New York: Viking Press.

Styron, W. 1990. *Darkness visible: A memoir of madness.* New York: Random House.

Swift, J. 1945. *Gulliver's travels.* New York: Grolier.

Tennyson, A. 1898. The poetic and dramatic works. Cambridge, Mass.: Houghton Mifflin.

Thomas, D. 1953. Do not go gentle into that good night. In *The collected poems of Dylan Thomas*. New York: New Directions.

Tillich, P. 1952. *The courage to be*. New Haven: Yale University.

Toffler, A. 1970. *Future shock*. New York: Random House.

Townsend, P. 1968. Isolation, desolation, and loneliness. In E. Shanas, P. Townsend, D. Wedderbury, H. Friis, P. Milkof, and G. Stehower, eds., *Old people in three industrial societies*. New York: Atherton Press.

Valliant, G. E. 1977. *Adaptation to life*. Boston: Little Brown.

Wallace, A. 1956. *Tornado in Worcester*. Washington, D.C.: National Academy of Sciences National Research Council.

Weisman, A. D. 1974. *The realization of death*. New York: Aronson.

Wickett, A. 1989. *Double exit*. Eugene, Ore.: Hemlock Society.

Williams, R. M., Jr. 1970. *American society*. New York: Alfred A. Knopf.

Acknowledgments

I thank Betty Booker for her support and encouragement and for her expert editorial suggestions and Margaret Flannagan for typing and proofreading the manuscript and for her patience. I am indebted to my husband, Ray, and my daughter, Cressida, for their patience and endurance during the writing of this book.

Index

About the Author

Nancy J. Osgood is associate professor of gerontology and sociology at Virginia Commonwealth University/Medical College of Virginia in Richmond, Virginia. She is the author of *Suicide in the Elderly: A Practitioner's Guide to Diagnosis and Mental Health Intervention;* co-author with John McIntosh of *Suicide and the Elderly: An Annotated Bibliography and Review;* and co-author with Barbara Brant and Aaron Lipman of *Suicide among the Elderly in Long-Term Care Facilities.* She has published numerous articles and has appeared on the *Oprah Winfrey Show, 60 Minutes,* and the *CBS Evening News.* Dr. Osgood is also the director of a statewide model program in Virginia for detection and prevention of alcoholism in older adults.